Homeschooling

# Brill Guides to Scholarship in Education

*Series Editors*

William M. Reynolds (*Georgia Southern University, USA*)
Brad Porfilio (*Seattle University, USA*)

*Editorial Board*

Donna Alvermann (*University of Georgia, USA*)
Antonia Darder (*Loyola Marymount University, USA*)
Petar Jandrić (*Tehničko veleučilište u Zagrebu, Croatia*)
Lagarrett J. King (*University of Missouri, USA*)
Sherell McArthur (*University of Georgia, USA*)
William F. Pinar (*University of British Columbia, Canada*)
Pauline Sameshima (*Lakehead University, Canada*)
Christine Sleeter (*California State University Monterey Bay, USA*)

VOLUME 6

The titles published in this series are listed at *brill.com/bgse*

# Homeschooling

*A Guidebook of Practices, Claims, Issues, and Implications*

*By*

T. Jameson Brewer

BRILL
SENSE

LEIDEN | BOSTON

All chapters in this book have undergone peer review.

Library of Congress Cataloging-in-Publication Data

Names: Brewer, T. Jameson, author.
Title: Homeschooling : a guidebook of practices, claims, issues, and
   implications / By T. Jameson Brewer.
Description: Leiden ; Boston : Brill | Sense, 2021. | Series: Brill guides
   to scholarship in education, 2590-1958 ; Volume 6 | Includes
   bibliographical references and index.
Identifiers: LCCN 2020057313 (print) | LCCN 2020057314 (ebook) | ISBN
   9789004457065 (paperback) | ISBN 9789004395954 (hardback) | ISBN
   9789004457096 (ebook)
Subjects: LCSH: Home schooling--United States--History. | Home
   schooling--Religious aspects--United States. | Education and
   state--United States. | School choice--United States.
Classification: LCC LC40 .B754 2021  (print) | LCC LC40  (ebook) | DDC
   371.04/2--dc23
LC record available at https://lccn.loc.gov/2020057313
LC ebook record available at https://lccn.loc.gov/2020057314

Typeface for the Latin, Greek, and Cyrillic scripts: "Brill". See and download: brill.com/brill-typeface.

ISSN 2590-1958
ISBN 978-90-04-45706-5 (paperback)
ISBN 978-90-04-39595-4 (hardback)
ISBN 978-90-04-45709-6 (e-book)

Copyright 2021 by Koninklijke Brill NV, Leiden, The Netherlands.
Koninklijke Brill NV incorporates the imprints Brill, Brill Hes & De Graaf, Brill Nijhoff, Brill Rodopi,
Brill Sense, Hotei Publishing, mentis Verlag, Verlag Ferdinand Schöningh and Wilhelm Fink Verlag.
All rights reserved. No part of this publication may be reproduced, translated, stored in a retrieval system,
or transmitted in any form or by any means, electronic, mechanical, photocopying, recording or otherwise,
without prior written permission from the publisher. Requests for re-use and/or translations must be
addressed to Koninklijke Brill NV via brill.com or copyright.com.

This book is printed on acid-free paper and produced in a sustainable manner.

# Contents

List of Illustrations  VII

1  Introduction  1

2  An Overview of the Homeschooling Landscape  18

3  Religious Rationales for Homeschooling  50

4  Political Rationales for Homeschooling  65

5  Claims of Effectiveness  74

6  Claims of Efficiency  85

7  Other Rationales & Conclusions  96

   Index  103

# Illustrations

### Figure

1.1  Homeschooling growth over time.  8

### Tables

1.1  Homeschooling growth over time.  8
1.2  Homeschooling by grade level.  9
1.3  Income of homeschooling families.  10
1.4  Parental employment among homeschooling families.  11
1.5  Number of children per homeschool.  11
1.6  Educational attainment of parents who homeschool.  11
2.1  Rationales over time.  20
6.1  Income and educational expenses (in 2019 dollars).  89
6.2  Cost over time.  91

CHAPTER 1

# Introduction

Homeschooling: the teaching of one's own children (or other children) at home. Generally, this is likely the image that is elicited in the minds of anyone picturing what it means to teach children at home rather than in traditional public schools. Though, while this simplistic understanding is mostly correct, the practice of educating children at home is not as cut and dry as one might expect. As will be explored, homeschooling – while done at home – is often an amalgamation of inputs and curriculum from varied sources (sometimes including resources from public schools and other public institutions such as libraries) and the rationales for such practices are often as varied. However, in whatever form or fashion homeschooling may take across the millions of homes that engage in the practice, a common theme among those families who homeschool are a belief that homeschools are better suited, better equipped, and more desirable to provide an education to their children than the professional teachers employed by traditional public schools.

There are a significant amount of questions that often arise surrounding homeschooling. For instance, who is being homeschooled? Who is doing the teaching at home? What, if any, credentials or training do homeschooling parents have? What curriculum is being used, for what purpose, and to what end? How might homeschooling aid or impede the socialization of children? How can the learning and progress of children be verified by colleges? What happens if a child is being abused or neglected? What are the rationales that parents use to justify homeschooling? And, relatedly, to what extent does parental sovereignty to make such decisions outweigh the obligation that society has towards its children? All of these questions are worth considering and the answers to each are likely to be as varied and heated as the next. This is especially true when it comes to questions about parental sovereignty. With little doubt, parents have unparalleled authority over the lives of their children when it comes to the broader society. Parents are able to choose which religion they will expose their children to (or not expose them to), parents are able to teach political values and moral values to their children with no oversight of any external force. Parents are able to decide how much screen time a child receives to how many potato chips a child eats. Indeed, there is no area small or large where parents are not the leading deciding factor in their child's lives. And, yet, our society would likely not function very well or for very long if it were comprised of nothing but disparate families making decisions that

© KONINKLIJKE BRILL NV, LEIDEN, 2021 | DOI: 10.1163/9789004457096_001

only impacted or affected them and their children with little regard for what it might mean for the broader society and collective good. Because of this we have decided, as a collective society, that there are, in fact, areas in a child's life in which parental sovereignty is rendered void when the life of a child is threatened due to abuse or neglect, for example. In these instances, the collective society – represented by the government – can go as far as to permanently remove a child from their parent's custody. Thankfully, this is a relatively rare process. But somewhere in the middle of supporting parental sovereignty to raise a child as a parent sees fit and the need for the broader society to continue to function exists the need for education. That is, there exists the need for future generations to have some shared sense of our collective past, our collective present, and have the necessary tools to work together towards a prosperous future. This was, in many ways, the rationale for the development of the common school as envisioned by Horace Mann. Children from all walks of life would come together to learn together for the betterment and maintenance of society. These common schools would be led by professional teachers who were vetted by society and who would teach a curriculum that was vetted and accountable to the local community, state, and federal government. Homeschooling exists in stark contrast to this understanding of education, teaching as a profession, and the collective benefits of schooling.

Homeschooling was, indeed, the first form of schooling that has long existed in the history of humankind. Early humans learned how to survive, hunt, gather, and later oversee agriculture from their parents. This early form of schooling ensured the survival of our species (though, it was likely done as a collective). As our societies have advanced, the education of children has likewise shifted. While the topic will be explored more thoroughly in the following chapter, the advancement of our societies necessitated the development of teaching as a profession to be done in a formal setting. Along similar lines, while homeschooling was the first form of education, homeopathy preceded professional medicine. As society developed further, it required the creation of a professional medical community with specialized knowledge to ensure the maintenance of that society – especially as that society grew larger in population. The medical profession itself, as a result of professionalizing, provides the necessary knowledge and insights into further medical advancement that, in turn, extends human life and the societies that such life makes up. While there are still families that prefer homeopathic remedies to maladies or using a string tied to a door to pull teeth, the vast majority of us understand that professional medicine and, in the case of teeth dentistry, is more ideal to ensure the health and wellbeing of each individual *and* the society, at large. Homeschooling, on the other hand, retains a conception of education that situates the practice as squarely focused on an individual student not the greater collective good and eschews notions that education is an important enough component of life to be overseen and delivered by trained professionals. In many ways, it is an intentional rejection of expertise and the very understandings that have fostered the development of our societies to this contemporary point. The continuation of anti-intellectualism and anti-professionalization of services offered by trained professionals in favor of parents providing such services relies heavily on the types of rationales that eschew doctor's visits and vaccines in favor of home remedies. Chief among these rationales is fear. Some parents engage in homeopathy in lieu of doctor visits and vaccines out of fear that vaccines, for example, will cause autism. These parents have convinced themselves that their "research" online through the University of Google justifies their fears and elevates their "insights" and "research" on medicine to equal, or surpass, the knowledge, training, insights, and research of physicians, medical colleges, laboratory researchers, and organizations such as the CDC and the WHO. In the cases where it is not entirely based on fear, the rationale seemingly includes hubris.

At the core of questions and discussions surrounding the practical operation of homeschooling and other forms of school choice (e.g., school vouchers, charter schools, virtual schools, "un-schooling," etc.) is: "By whom, for whom, and to what end do we engage in this thing called schooling?" The answers to these complex questions are often nuanced and complicated. For many, schooling, regardless of the delivery system, represents an opportunity for their children to engage in a seemingly required process of credentialism that informs future economic opportunities (Labaree, 1997). For others, it represents an opportunity for pure learning; what we might call a liberal education. And, still again, many understand schooling as a combination of these two rationales. Questions surrounding the purpose of schooling often center on how and why students should be socialized into society – both in terms of the social aspects of interacting with other individuals but also specific socialization into our nation's civics, history, and political systems. Many students, conversely, often suggest that they attend schools because they are forced to attend under compulsory laws and parents who, understandably so, do not want to be fined or imprisoned. And to this latter point, the implementation of compulsory education laws across the country following the creation of the common school suggests, to some extent, a framework for answering some of the above questions and rationales; which, admittedly, is not an exhaustive list. The very nature of compulsory schooling at the threat of criminal prosecution for parents who fail to enroll their children in some type of education suggests that our society places a great deal of importance on schooling. Our society holds education in such high importance that we mandate, as a collective, that every single individual child engage in learning often until a predetermined age where a child and/or the parent can opt-out of the compulsory requirement. This predetermined age is state-based and, thus, varies across the country. The rationale behind compulsory education is one of the most central tenets of the stability of a nation and social cohesion (or at the very least, social control) (Urban & Wagoner, 2009). And while the government enforces its compulsory attendance laws on threat of punitive consequences should a parent not have their children participate, the required participation is not limited to schools that are run by the government – also known as public schools. In fact, in all 50 states, while parents are required to ensure that their children are engaging in some type of educative experience, it need not be limited to public schools as parents can opt to send their children to private schools, charter schools, or participate in homeschooling.

The varying options for schooling represent an insight into how individual families, and the nation as a whole, interpret the question regarding to what end and for whose purpose is education. Regardless of how a family might understand education in terms of its ability to provide credentials for future economic stability or for college and career training, the type of schooling that a parent places their child in can be telling of how the parent interprets the broader goals of education. Namely, regardless of the rationales for homeschooling a child, the practice represents understanding education as a specifically individual process, designed for an individual, and to the ends that it benefits the individual. This, in my view, is the epitome of the type of "pull oneself up by your bootstraps" disposition endemic within notions of meritocracy. It is the "I'm going to focus on what's best for me" and, if everyone else did that, everyone would be fine philosophy of society.

While questions surrounding the claims of who is best suited to provided such an education is worthwhile (a topic taken up in Chapter 2), I want to focus more broadly here on what schooling outside of public education means, writ large. To do this, we must first understand public schools as a mechanism, process, location, and entity that reinforces notions of social cohesion and understands the purpose of education as not only beneficial to the individual student but, taken as a whole, beneficial to the student's class, grade level, school, community, state, and nation. Each individual student is understood as vitally important to the broader community such that we provide for a fully funded (in theory), free at the point of delivery, public education for every child. Public schooling understands that the education of one student will pay community and societal dividends both in terms of a national identity but also economically. Specifically, we understand that investment in public schools is one of the best returns on investments that the government can make because the investment in the individual benefits the collective. In short, the individual education of a student is understood, specifically, as a benefit to that individual but also to the broader collective good. Comparatively, publicly funded firefighting services are obviously beneficial to an individual family if their house were to catch fire. Yet, publicly funded firefighting is also understood as a public and common good because a fire extinguished at one house prevents it from spreading to another, but also, the loss of a singular home in the community represents a communal financial, social, and emotional burden that often exceeds the costs of maintaining a fire brigade. The cost of educating a child in public schools is far lower than the financial, social, and emotional costs associated with a society supplementing an uneducated adult later in life. Moreover, the founding fathers understood public education as a necessary means to ensure that citizens were capable of engaging in our republic, thus leading us eventually to compulsory attendance laws. Moreover, because the education of the future generation is vital to that generations own well-being as individuals and as a collective, compulsory attendance laws ensure that children – who often cannot manifest their own volition in their rearing – are actually being given the opportunity to learn that may, or may not, be occurring if each family decides whether or not their children will have any education at all.

Running counter to this philosophy of schooling as both an individual and collective good are private schools, charter schools, and homeschooling. Each of these forms of schooling represent, in part or in whole, the assertion that the education of an individual child is for the sake of the individual child as an understanding of a broader commitment and benefit to the collective good is either ignored or is specifically marginalized as socialist, communist, or statist (Ray, 2016). In many ways, the suggestion that education and schooling be understood as both a benefit to the individual as well as the collective good is scoffed at as an attack on individual liberty and freedoms. Yet, each of us as individuals have a social and moral obligation to ensure that future generations are capable and adequately prepared to integrate into our society as adults. And recoiling from this social obligation in favor of rugged individualism threatens a social cohesion that requires individuals to remain true to their own values but, simultaneously, respect and integrate the views – or the opportunity for those views – of others into our daily lives from the minutiae of social interactions to the development of federal policies that become enforceable laws. Put another way, "If school attendance is considered important to social integration, non-attendance through home education can be viewed as a threat to integration" (Beck, 2015, p. 87). Beck goes on to note that,

> Van Galen distinguishes between ideological and pedagogic home educators. Ideological home educators emphasize family values and conservative values and are motivated by disagreement with schools as to values; they are often loosely referred to as religious fundamentalists. Pedagogic home educators consider that they can pursue more desirable pedagogic approaches outside the schools system. The intensity of the home educator's motivation may be a reflection of his or her sense of conflict with society at large. For some, home education is an act of conscience in a secularized society and secularized schools. The US sociologist Steven distinguishes between heaven-based and earth-based drives for homeschooling. The heaven-based category expresses motivations that are mainly matters of principle, religion and life view and adherence to ideological pedagogic approaches. According to Stevens, earth-based home educators are acting on situation-specific, pragmatic and other specifically pedagogic issues. (Beck, 2015, p. 89)

Thus, the recoiling away from understanding the power of public schools to ensure the ability of society to realize social cohesion and progress in favor of elevating a sense of "what is best for me and me alone" is part, of the rationale of opting for some type of private individualized schooling. Because society has a responsibility to ensure that children are able to function in society by the time they become adults, we likewise have a shared responsibility to ensure that children are afforded the opportunity of a diverse socialization experience towards these ends (Lubienski & Brewer, 2014). In fact, "Schools' most important tasks were to level out societal differences and to implement social integration" (Beck, 2015). However, as was suggested above, there are some (including but not limited to the homeschooling movement) that argue that such a societal commitment is a "statist belief system" akin to Marxism (Ray, 2016). In this way, believing that society has a shared commitment to all children is understood as a threat to libertarianism, rugged individualism, and private property within a deregulated capitalistic market economy.

No movement is without its organizations. There are two overarching national organizations dedicated to providing assistance and resources for homeschooling families and in the effort to promote the practice. The first is the HSLDA that operates as both a legal consulting agency providing advice for homeschooling families and as an advocacy group pressing for the preservation and expansion of laws favorable to homeschooling.

The second is the National Home Education Research Institute (NHERI) that serves as a clearinghouse for research conducted on homeschooling and

"specializes in homeschool research, facts, statistics, scholarly articles, and information" (NHERI, n.d.). Among the facts and statistics on homeschooling is the rationale for why a parent chooses to educate their children at home rather than participate in public education. According to the NHERI, the most common rationales for why parents homeschool their children are:
– customize or individualize the curriculum and learning environment for each child,
– accomplish more academically than in schools,
– use pedagogical approaches other than those typical in institutional schools,
– enhance family relationships between children and parents and among siblings,
– provide guided and reasoned social interactions with youthful peers and adults,
– provide a safer environment for children and youth, because of physical violence, drugs and alcohol, psychological abuse, racism, and improper and unhealthy sexuality associated with institutional schools, and,
– teach and impart a particular set of values, beliefs, and worldview to children and youth (Ray, 2019).

As will be explored in greater detail later, it is often the case that homeschooling advocates position rationales of individualized curriculum and, seemingly, "better" pedagogical techniques (despite limited to no regulation on credentialing or oversight of who teaches at home) over what seem to be the more prevalent rationale: the last point listed above.

## 1 What the Homeschool Community Looks Like

According to the NHERI, there are, as of late 2019, approximately 2.5 million students being homeschooled in the United States. The NHERI estimates that the total population of students who are homeschooled grows by 2% to 8% annually and, as such, represents the "fastest-growing form of education in the United States" (Ray, 2019). Data from the National Center for Education Statistics is shown in Table 1.1. In sum, of the school-aged students in the United States, approximately 3% are homeschooled (NCES, n.d.) and have largely leveled off over the past few years (see Figure 1.1).

According to the data available from the NCES, White families still remain the largest demographic within the homeschooling community despite a relative reduction in the amount of Whites who homeschool over the past

TABLE 1.1  Homeschooling growth over time

|          | 1999    | 2003      | 2007      | 2012      | 2016      |
|----------|---------|-----------|-----------|-----------|-----------|
| Total    | 850,000 | 1,096,000 | 1,520,000 | 1,773,000 | 1,690,000 |
| White    | 640,000 | 843,000   | 1,171,000 | 1,205,000 | 998,000   |
| Black    | 84,000  | 103,000   | 61,000    | 140,000   | 132,000   |
| Hispanic | 77,000  | 59,000    | 147,000   | 265,000   | 444,000   |

SOURCE: NCES (N.D.)

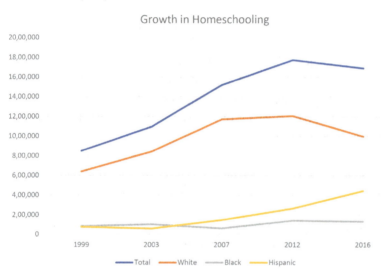

FIGURE 1.1  Homeschooling growth over time

few years. NCES data suggests that the total amount of White students being homeschooled in 2016 was down nearly to the total population in 2007. Comparatively, the fastest growing racial demographic to homeschool is that of the Hispanic community who experienced a 652% growth between 2003 and 2016 in the total number of Hispanic families that homeschool.

Between 1999 and 2003, the total population of homeschooled students grew by 29%, then grew by 39% between 2003 and 2007, then experienced a slowdown as it grew only by 17% between 2007 and 2012, and finally saw a negative 5% reduction between 2012 and 2016. However, even with a recent reduction in the total number of students being homeschooled, the total number of students being educated at home doubled between 1999 and 2016. Considering the relative size of the practice to that of all K-12 aged students in the United States, 1.7% were homeschooled in 1999, 2.2% in 2003, 3.0% in 2007, 3.4% in 2009, and 3.6% in 2016.

INTRODUCTION

The NHERI estimates that in addition to the 2.3 million students currently being homeschooled (it is important to note here that NCES data ends at 2016 and may account for the discrepancy between the estimation numbers of NCES and NHERI), 3.4 million individuals have previously been homeschooled at some point in their lives, bringing the total number of Americans that experienced some type of homeschooling to 5.7 million (Ray, 2019).

The age, or grade level, of homeschooled students vary but by and large the majority of children being homeschooled in the United States are in Kindergarten through 5th grade (see Table 1.2).

TABLE 1.2    Homeschooling by grade level

|  | 1999 | 2003 | 2007 | 2012 | 2016 |
|---|---|---|---|---|---|
| K–5 | 428,000 | 472,000 | 717,000 | 833,000 | 767,000 |
| K | 92,000 | – | – | 212,000 | 181,000 |
| 1–3 | 199,000 | 214,000 | 406,000 | 353,000 | 300,000 |
| 4–5 | 136,000 | 160,000 | 197,000 | 268,000 | 287,000 |
| 6–8 | 186,000 | 302,000 | 371,000 | 424,000 | 398,000 |
| 9–12 | 235,000 | 315,000 | 422,000 | 516,000 | 525,000 |

SOURCE: NCES (N.D.)

Brian Ray of the NHERI estimates that the average amount of time that students are homeschooled is between 6 and 8 years. And, as an aside, this is an important fact. While many within homeschooling advocacy organizations and groups tout homeschooling as the reason for good academic outcomes, we know that the majority of homeschooled students are not homeschooled for the entirety of their K-12 experience and do just as well academically in their public school settings. This tells us more about the impact of the type of student and the family's socioeconomic status that homeschools rather than the form of schooling such students attend. As suggested below and taken up in greater detail in subsequent chapters, the family's economic reality is the largest informant of academic outcomes and because homeschooling families are, on average, significantly more affluent, their children do well in both the homeschool and public school environment.

But why have nearly six million individuals been educated at home? Again, while the rationale of imparting a specific, often narrow, world view (e.g., politics and religion) are among the greatest reason families homeschool, claims of greater effectiveness are pervasive among homeschooling advocates and practitioners. The claim, as it goes, is that homeschooling relative to public schools is able to produce better academic outcomes on achievement tests and college acceptance. Accordingly, the NHERI claims that students who are homeschooled score 15 to 30 points higher on standardized achievement tests when compared to their public school counterparts (Ray, 2019).

However, all of these claims are likely the result of the logical fallacy of seeking to find causation with correlation. That is, the question that should be asked here is "is the practice of homeschooling itself, rather than other factors or influences, causing the relative difference in outcomes and attainment? In comparing homeschooling students to those students who are educated at public schools may very well fall victim to a classical apples to oranges comparison that overlooks some significant environmental, economic, and family realities that may be better situated to help explain the variance in outcomes and attainment. The impact of a family's socioeconomic status on student educational outcomes has long been studied, documented, and understood to be the driving factor in determining or predicting outcomes (Bowles & Gintis, 1976; Brewer & Myers, 2015; Carter & Welner, 2013; Coleman, 1990; Coleman et al., 1966; Ennis, 1976; Jencks & Phillips, 1998; Jencks et al., 1972; Ladson-Billings, 2006; Rothstein, 2004; Wilkinson & Pickett, 2010). While it will be explored in greater detail in Chapter 7, the median household income for families that homeschool is $94,083 and is disaggregated in Table 1.3.

TABLE 1.3    Income of homeschooling families

|  | 1999 | 2003 | 2007 | 2012 | 2016 |
|---|---|---|---|---|---|
| $20,000 or less | 184,000 | 164,000 | 186,000 | 219,000 | 184,000 |
| $20,001 to $50,000 | 356,000 | 430,000 | 420,000 | 528,000 | 483,000 |
| $50,001 to $75,000 | 162,000 | 264,000 | 414,000 | 370,000 | 435,000 |
| $75,001 to $100,000 | 148,000 | 169,000 | 264,000 | 288,000 | 268,000 |
| Over $100,000 | – | – | 236,000 | 367,000 | 319,000 |

SOURCE: NCES (N.D.)

Related to income is the employment status of the adults in families who homeschool. It is of little surprise that the vast majority of families who homeschool have only one parent in the labor force as the practice of homeschooling requires one parent to remain at home to facilitate the homeschool (see Table 1.4).

The majority of homeschooling families across the United States have three or more children as a family (see Table 1.3). This reality aligns with the quiverfull philosophy as explored in Chapter 3.

INTRODUCTION                                                                          11

TABLE 1.4    Parental employment among homeschooling families

|                                      | 1999    | 2003    | 2007    | 2012    | 2016    |
|--------------------------------------|---------|---------|---------|---------|---------|
| Two parents (both) in labor force    | 237,000 | 274,000 | 518,000 | 588,000 | 427,000 |
| Two parents, one in labor force      | 444,000 | 594,000 | 808,000 | 719,000 | 935,000 |
| One parent, in work force            | 98,000  | 174,000 | 127,000 | 247,000 | 189,000 |
| No parent working                    | 71,000  | —       | —       | 130,000 | 139,000 |

SOURCE: NCES (N.D.)

TABLE 1.5    Number of children per homeschool

|                 | 1999    | 2003    | 2007    | 2012    | 2016    |
|-----------------|---------|---------|---------|---------|---------|
| One child       | 132,000 | 110,000 | 197,000 | 418,000 | 338,000 |
| Two children    | 248,000 | 306,000 | 414,000 | 493,000 | 475,000 |
| Three or more   | 470,000 | 679,000 | 909,000 | 862,000 | 877,000 |

SOURCE: NCES (N.D.)

TABLE 1.6.    Educational attainment of parents who homeschool

|                                    | 1999    | 2003    | 2007    | 2012    | 2016    |
|------------------------------------|---------|---------|---------|---------|---------|
| HS diploma or less                 | 160,000 | 269,000 | 208,000 | 560,000 | 510,000 |
| Voc/Tech, AA, some college         | 287,000 | 338,000 | 559,000 | 525,000 | 418,000 |
| Bachelor's/some graduate school    | 213,000 | 309,000 | 444,000 | 434,000 | 501,000 |
| Graduate/professional degree       | 190,000 | 180,000 | 309,000 | 255,000 | 260,000 |

SOURCE: NCES (N.D.)

As explored in greater detail in Chapter 2, the qualifications of parents who homeschool is among the chief concerns and critiques associated with the practice. Namely, what are the educational credentials of those adults leading the education of children? Table 1.6 explicates the educational attainment of those parents who facilitate the education of their children. Of interest here is that the majority of parents who lead homeschooling in the United States have a high school diploma, or less. While the number of parents who homeschool their children with a college degree has, at times, outnumbered those parents with a high school diploma or less, the last decade has seen a dramatic increase in the number of parents who have no more than a high school diploma (or less) as the teacher of record for their children.

## 2    Homeschooling as School Choice

While the practice of homeschooling has long been in existence prior to, and throughout, the growth and expansion of public schools overseen by the local, state, and federal governments, homeschooling is now understood as an option within the larger umbrella of school choice. The school choice movement takes on many forms: charter schools, private schools, "un-schooling," online schools, and homeschooling. In some cases, these choices reflect a pure rejection of public engagement (both in terms of learning and funding) in favor of a private choice. For example, a family that choses to forgo enrolling their children in a local public school while opting to enroll them in a parochial private school while paying for the tuition entirely on their own has exercised what I will call, here, a pure schooling choice. That is, the family is choosing to not participate or engage in the public education option and is providing the funding of that alternative choice entirely on their own. Mixed school choice can take on many iterations. Online schooling, for example, can be a partnership or collaboration with a traditional public school or can be a method of schooling overseen and delivered by a charter school company (either nonprofit or for-profit). In some of these instances, the choice to educate a child at home represents a mixture of choice in that some of the educative experiences are facilitated by a public entity (which would, of course, include public funding) which may include interaction with public school teachers and other public school students (either in a virtual classroom setting or through in-person extracurricular activities at the local public school). Other school choice scenarios that constitute a mixture of choice, as I define it here, are instances of families receiving some type of public funding to help offset the costs associated with their private/individual education choice. For example, there are many states that provide tax-credits or state-level tax deductions for families that homeschool their children or send their children to private schools. In these instances, families are able to reduce their overall tax liability with the state by a pre-determined amount. As is often the case, state-level tax laws across the states vary on how this loss of state tax income is handled or offset. Nevertheless, in states that provide tax deductions or credits, the family that engages in the school choice option of homeschooling results in a reduction of collected state taxes which, in turn, blur the lines of costs associated with the exercise of school choice.

INTRODUCTION 13

School choice mechanisms where the family engaging in the private choice of education results in the transfer portions of, or the entire, allocation of public funds into private hands likewise represents a mixture of choice – albeit, a decidedly more problematic one. School voucher mechanisms that allow students to not only enact the practice of school choice by not registering for a local public school but rather at a private school but to shift larger portions (or the entire portion) of the federal and state education spending allocation per student is the epitome of an individual family exercising school choice while other families pay the price with public funds. States that allow for a school voucher to represent the full amount of allocated funds that were slated to be delivered to a local public school not only deprive the public school of those funds – which, taken in large sum help offset the costs associated with educating the remaining children – but those funds are often placed into the hands of private entities. This siphoning off of public funds into the hands of private organizations becomes further problematic when you consider that the majority of private schools are parochial in nature – thus violating the federal Establishment Clause and state-level Blaine Amendments. In 2019, the Georgia legislature put forth a bill that would have allowed the full per-student amount of federal and state dollars allocated for public schools to be moved over to offset the costs associated with private school tuition. The move would have shifted $48 million away from public schools in its first year, rising to as high as $543 million in 10 years (Brewer, 2019). Yet, as is often the case surrounding school choice, parents who want to exercise choice often claim "it's my kid, it's my tax money" as a combination of parental sovereignty and public policy justification. However, while parental sovereignty is a worthwhile topic (taken up in Chapter 2), the majority of parents do not pay anywhere near the annual cost of educating their child through their own taxes. In 2016, the state of Georgia spent an average of $9,769 per student per year while the median property tax paid by families was $1,346 which, of course, not all of the taxes paid went exclusively to school budgets (Brewer, 2019). As such, the cost to educate one child in Georgia in 2016 required the property taxes of 7.2 families (assuming all of the tax money collected went to schools, which again, it doesn't). In practice, then, school choice mechanisms that shift the full amount of funds that are allocated for public education into the hands of private organizations or families homeschooling would require that at least 6 other families subsidize the costs while having no oversight while simultaneously reducing the funds available to local public schools. In no other aspect of public funding for public services does this phenomenon exist. A proposal by an individual to shift tax money allocated for the local police department to offset the costs associated with private home security would never be entertained by society. Similarly, a

14 CHAPTER 1

proposal to shift tax money allocated for public parks to offset the costs of a private country club membership would, likewise, never be entertained, supported, or approved by the general public. However, when it comes to the phenomenon of school choice, such proposals are not only entertained, they are often celebrated as an artifact of 'American freedom.'

## 3 Unique Times

Of interest to the critique and overview of homeschooling that follows in this text is the context in which the book found its final editing. In March of 2020, all public schools in the United States were closed indefinitely as a response to the COVID-19 pandemic that swept the globe. The shuttering of public schools in favor of online and digital learning at home, in many ways, created a new environment under which all students in the country were, for a time, being homeschooled. While this type of homeschooling is not to be understood as fully synonymous with the traditional types of homeschooling that will be explored here, it would be wrong to suggest that there were not similarities. For me, what becomes most apparent in the quarantined homeschool environment brought about by COVID-19 is quite precisely one of the factors that led many schools to delay or struggle with the thought of closing their doors. Namely, moving public education to an online, at-home, setting brought a magnifying glass onto the socioeconomic disparities surrounding education and who can, and cannot, afford to educate their children at home. As will be explored in greater detail in subsequent chapters, the option of homeschooling one's children relies heavily on a vast amount of financial capacity that is unlike the typical American family. Put bluntly, traditional homeschooling is largely done by affluent families who can afford to forgo a parental income to allow a parent to remain at home to teach their children. In the COVID-19 context, families across the country were left with the harrowing prospect of losing jobs they could not afford to lose because their children would be at home when they would otherwise be at school. For those students who rely on free and reduced lunch programs, the shuttering of schools represents an ongoing and daily threat to their wellbeing given a lack of access to food. Despite the learning-at-home as a result of COVID-19, what also differed is that K-12 students were still being taught by professional teachers, just from a distance. While digital learning is not without its own problems (Anderson, 2018), the content and curriculum students worked through was still the result of expert and professional pedagogues. Other troublesome patters that the temporary nation-wide schooling-at-home exposed was a decrease

INTRODUCTION

in reporting of child abuse. Specifically, because public schools serve as community oversight as "teachers and administrators are often the first ones to see the signs of abuse," the closing of public schools in light of the pandemic led to a 50% decrease in child abuse reporting (Prabhu, 2020). This trend was documented across the country raising significant concerns from social workers and child advocates who noted that, "when children are no longer visible to the vast majority of people who are trained and required to report, and then you see this kind of decline [in reported cases], we get super concerned" (LeBlanc, 2020).

This time also found, at least from my anecdotal observations, a growing repertoire of tongue-in-cheek memes shared on social media by both teachers and parents reflecting on the likelihood that society would have a new found appreciation for the work that professional educators do on a daily basis. So, while COVID-19 temporarily situated all students in the United States as students educated at home, it perfectly highlighted the disparities in our education system that are a result of socioeconomic stratification and the relative privileges of those families who are able to, and do, homeschool their children on a regular and ongoing basis. For example, there were 21.3 million Americans in 2019 who did not have access to broadband internet at home and a full one-third of all rural homes with no internet connection at all and that, overall, low-income households have "lower levels of technology adoption" (Greene, 2020). Peter Greene goes on to conclude that if you are thinking,

> well, school can just happen at home and there will be nothing to worry about," think again. Beyond all the "hilarious" memes about the home school teacher drinking too much or wanting to pay teachers a zillion dollars, lies the truth that doing school at home is hard no matter how you do it, and not everyone is well-equipped to tackle it. It is certainly not a great way to deliver on the promise of a free, full education for every single student. If this crisis is going to drag on too much longer, we're going to need a better, more complete solution than just "go home and do some school there. (Greene, 2020)

So, while the nation turned to temporary homeschooling (more appropriately described as schooling-at-home since curriculum and lessons were being provided and facilitated by professional educators) during the pandemic crisis that began in the spring of 2020, it was wrought with problems and, as Greene suggests, not only highlights the disparities among the have's and have not's but raises significant questions about the quality of learning at home for all children. In what follows, we explore these questions further.

## 4 Overview of This Book

Chapter 2 of this text explores, in further detail, the historical practice of homeschooling through the contemporary period. Chapter 3 takes up the rationale of religion as a reason that many parents homeschool while Chapter 4 explores those rationales more closely associated with what I'll call politics. The notion of, and questions surrounding, claims of effectiveness offered by homeschooling are explored in Chapter 5 while claims of homeschooling efficiencies are taken up in Chapter 6 followed by other rationales and some concluding thoughts in Chapter 7.

## References

Anderson, M. (2018). *Humanization in the digital age: A critique of technophilia in education* (PhD dissertation). Georgia State University, Atlanta, GA. https://scholarworks.gsu.edu/eps_diss/183/?fbclid=IwAR0dBmAauiQwv3 DoIsa4wBNwhoegXNWoNYRxas2vZovcxlyy-2DElm2pqvs

Beck, C. W. (2015). Home education and social integration In P. Rothermel (Ed.), *International perspectives on home education: Do we still need schools?* (pp. 87–98). Palgrave.

Bowles, S., & Gintis, H. (1976). *Schooling in capitalist America*. Harper Collins.

Brewer, T. J. (2019). *Opinion: Voucher bill is not 'neutral.' It will hurt Georgia public schools*. Retrieved February 6, 2020, from https://www.ajc.com/blog/get-schooled/ opinion-voucher-bill-not-neutral-will-hurt-georgia-public-schools/ 1zFwybpjuhGBvosJnJBrCJ/

Brewer, T. J., & Myers, P. S. (2015). How neoliberalism subverts equality and perpetuates poverty in our nation's schools. In S. N. Haymes, M. V. d. Haymes, & R. Miller (Eds.), *The Routledge handbook of poverty in the United States* (pp. 190–198). Routledge.

Carter, P. L., & Welner, K. G. (Eds.). (2013). *Closing the opportunity gap: What America must do to give every child and even chance*. Oxford University Press.

Coleman, J. (1990). *Equality and achievement in education*. Westview Press.

Coleman, J., Campbell, E. Q., Hobson, C. J., McPartland, J., Mood, A. M., Weinfeld, F. D., & York, R. L. (1966). *Equality of educational opportunity*. Department of Health, Education, and Welfare.

Ennis, R. H. (1976). Equality of educational opportunity. *Educational Theory, 26*(1), 3–18.

Greene, P. (2020). *Coronavirus forces schooling from home. Why that will be a problem*. Retrieved March 20, 2020, from https://www.forbes.com/sites/petergreene/2020/ 03/19/coronavirus-forces-schooling-from-home-why-that-will-be-a-problem/ #264cf00a1162

Jencks, C., & Phillips, M. (Eds.). (1998). *The Black-White test score gap*. Brookings Institution Press.

Jencks, C., Smith, M., Acland, H., Bane, M. J., Cohen, D., Gintis, H., ... Michelson, S. (1972). *Inequality: A reassessment of the effect of family and schooling in America*. Basic Books, Inc.

Labaree, D. (1997). *How to succeed in school without really learning: The credentials race in American education*. Yale University Press.

Ladson-Billings, G. (2006). From the achievement gap to the education debt: Understanding achievement in U.S. Schools. *Educational Researcher, 35*(7), 3–12.

LeBlanc, P. (2020). *Child abuse reports are down during the pandemic. Experts say that's a bad sign*. Retrieved May 17, 2020, from https://www.cnn.com/2020/05/17/politics/child-abuse-pandemic/index.html

Lubienski, C., & Brewer, T. J. (2014). Does home education "work"? Challenging the assumptions behind the home education movement. In P. Rothermel (Ed.), *International perspectives on home education: Do we still need schools?* (pp. 136–147). Palgrave.

NCES. (n.d.). *Homeschooling*. Retrieved December 3, 2019, from https://nces.ed.gov/fastfacts/display.asp?id=91

NHERI. (n.d.). *About NHERI*. Retrieved December 5, 2019, from https://www.nheri.org/about-nheri/

Prabhu, M. T. (2020). *Child abuse reporting in Georgia down by half since schools closed amid virus*. Retrieved April 16, 2020, from https://www.ajc.com/news/state--regional-govt--politics/child-abuse-reporting-georgia-down-half-since-schools-closed-amid-virus/RKg3HzBy86Ai3QNq3jrZML/

Ray, B. D. (2016). Introduction to recent changes and research in us homeschooling. In B. S. Cooper, F. R. Spielhagen, & C. Ricci (Eds.), *Homeschooling in new view* (2nd ed., pp. 3–28). Information Age.

Ray, B. D. (2019). Research facts on homeschooling. Retrieved August 5, 2019, from https://www.nheri.org/research-facts-on-homeschooling/

Rothstein, R. (2004). *Class and schools: Using social, economic, and educational reform to close the Black-White achievement gap*. Economic Policy Institute.

Urban, W. J., & Wagoner, J. L. (2009). *American education: A history* (4th ed.). Routledge.

Wilkinson, R., & Pickett, K. (2010). *The spirit level: Why greater equality makes societies stronger*. Bloomsbury Press.

CHAPTER 2

# An Overview of the Homeschooling Landscape

Homeschooling in its various forms is, without question, the oldest form of semi-formal education throughout all of the history of humanity. Adults have been teaching their children for thousands of years all manner of survival knowledge dating back to early humans such as hunting, gathering, and defense from predators to agricultural knowledge with the advent of the agricultural revolution in Mesopotamia. I refer to this as semi-formal rather than formal education in the sense that such training and skills transfer was done not only as an imperative for survival but often done so in the action of addressing immediate needs and not, necessarily, done in a structured environment (structured homeschooling or otherwise). That is, this teaching and learning was not understood as a formalized process where specific time, goals, and agendas were targeted and met. The teaching here falls along the normal teaching that parents do in the daily efforts to socialize their children into the norms of a particular family, language, culture, geographic region, etc. The historical and legal basis for homeschooling in the United States rests in the Supreme Court decisions of *Meyer v. Nebraska* (1926) and *Pierce v. Society of Sisters* (1925). Those cases concluded that "the state does not have the power to 'standardize its children by forcing them to accept instruction from public teachers only'" (Kunzman, 2012, p. 77) and that parents have a natural – though, not constitutional – right to decide the type of education their children receive. This lack of an explicit constitutional right is at odds with the prevailing assertion following these cases that the natural rights of the parent (or parental sovereignty) supersede the need of such legal rights. Specifically, while the U.S. Constitution does not explicitly afford children the right to an education (though, most state Constitutions do as does the United Nation's Declaration of Human Rights) and all states require compulsory attendance at some type of schooling (by and large, public schools), the ascendancy of parental sovereignty over such laws continues to establish the conception of parental control as not only natural but above some conceptions of international, federal, and state laws. This is not exclusive to homeschooling as many states allow parents to opt-out of legally mandated vaccination schedules sometimes on a whim following the development of ideology suspicious of vaccines after viewing YouTube videos of celebrities who are champions of the anti-vaccination movement. And while my intent here is not to challenge the role that parents do, and should, play in the lives of their children, the

© KONINKLIJKE BRILL NV, LEIDEN, 2021 | DOI: 10.1163/9789004457096_002

question becomes to what extent do individual choices made to benefit individual children (whether those choices are good or negligent) impact those children themselves and others in both the immediate sense but in a long-term societal sense.

Here, then, it becomes necessary to question role of homeschooling in the United States in terms of where the line is, should be (or should not be), drawn between semi-formal socialization overseen by parents and more formal education delivered and administrated by professionals, overseen by the state (the formal collective voice of society). At odds here is an overarching debate about the role of parental sovereignty and striking a balance between such sovereignty (a decidedly individual approach and administration of socialization) and each family's broader commitment and obligation to the common good – and the function of the common good (the public/state) to help ensure the transmission of its own civic culture and ensuring that children are being provided an ample opportunity towards adulthood that naturally follows appropriate educational and growth development.

## 1 Why Homeschool?

Generally speaking, there are two overarching rationales for why parents will chose to homeschool their children. And while my intention here is not to fit all parents into a box or generalize, it is worth categorizing rationales so that a discussion and assessment can follow. There are two broad categories that can explain rationales to homeschool: "(1) empirical – claims of greater efficiency, effectiveness, or pedagogical appropriateness; and (2) ideological – often informed by a religious or political disposition" (Brewer & Lubienski, 2017, p. 22). Each of these two broad categorizations of rationales can be subdivided into underlying assumptions, dispositions, and ideologies about curriculum, student development, assessment strategies, individualized instruction, addressing students with disabilities, beliefs about the broader culture in society, thoughts of bullying and other issues related to real or perceived threats to safety, beliefs about the role of science in relation to religion (e.g., creationism versus evolution), stances on sex education, political beliefs about the role of government in schools, indoctrination, and conspiracy theories that can, at times, provide an intersection for political and religious beliefs – quite often becoming dangerous (Westover, 2018).

In its 2012 survey, the Department of Education found that "nine in 10 homeschooled students' parents reported that concern about schools' environments was an important reason for their decision to homeschool"

TABLE 2.1    Rationales over time

|  | 1999 | 2003 | | 2012 | | 2016 | |
|---|---|---|---|---|---|---|---|
|  |  | Important | Most Important | Important | Most Important | Important | Most Important |
| A desire to provide religious instruction | 38.4% |  |  | 64% | 17% | 51% | 16% |
| A desire to provide moral instruction | 15.1% | 72.3% | 29.8% | 77% | 5% | 67% | 5% |
| A concern about the environment of other schools, such as safety, drugs, or negative peer pressure | 25.6% | 85.4% | 31.2% | 91% | 25% | 80% | 34% |
| A dissatisfaction with the academic instruction at other schools | 48.9%[a] 12.1%[b] 11.5%[c] | 68.2% | 16.5% | 74% | 19% | 61% | 17% |
| A desire to provide a nontraditional approach to child's education | 11.6%[d] |  |  | 44% | 5% | 39% | 6% |

(cont.)

TABLE 2.1    Rationales over time (*cont.*)

| | 1999 | 2003 | | 2012 | | 2016 | |
|---|---|---|---|---|---|---|---|
| | | Important | Most Important | Important | Most Important | Important | Most Important |
| Child has other special needs | 8.2% | 28.9% | 7.2% | 16% | – | 20% | 6% |
| Child has a physical or mental health problem | | 15.9% | 6.5% | 15% | 5% | 14% | 6% |
| Other reasons (e.g., family time, finances, travel, and distance) | 16.8% | 20.1% | 8.8% | 37% | 21% | 22% | 11% |

a  "Can give child better education at home."

b  "Object to what school teaches."

c  "Other problems with available schools."

d  "School does not challenge child."

SOURCE: ADAPTED FROM CUI AND HANSON (2019); PRINCIOTTA, BIELICK, AND CHAPMAN (2006); REDFORD ET AL. (2017)

(Redford, Battle, Bielick, & Grady, 2017, p. 11). Table 2.1 represents a compilation of statistics related to parental rationales to homeschool over time. In the surveys conducted by the National Center for Education Statistics (NCES) (where the data in Table 2.1 is derived from), parents could select one or more rationales.

As explicated in Table 2.1, the largest rationale provided as the "most important" reason for choosing to homeschool is "a concern about the environment of schools." While "a desire to provide religious instruction" is among the highest rationales reported, it is not unreasonable to assume that many of the rationales related to concerns about school environments or "dissatisfaction with the academic instruction" are, perhaps, informed by religious doctrine as homeschooling is seen by some as "one of the last opportunities to teach our children the unpolluted truth. If the public schools continue down their current path, Christians, conservatives and those who simply fear for their child's safety are going to start withdrawing their children" (Schillinger, Ray, Knapp, & Newman, n.d.).

Before we explore more specific claims about the negative influences of public education that are often promoted to support the growth of homeschooling, a brief aside as a way to provide context for how these claims take on a life of their own. In the 1962 film *The Music Man*, a seminal scene depicts the intentional and viral development of a myth and fear mongering surrounding the installation of a new billiards table in the local pool hall. Harold Hill (played by Robert Preston) notes the need to "create a problem," and "create a need" for his boy choir by creating and perpetuating myths surrounding how the game of billiards would result in the moral decay of the children in River City, the townspeople quickly adopt the belief that the new billiards table and the pool hall represent an existential threat to children. Lubienski and Lubienski (2014) also noted *The Music Man* as an example of expressing precisely how motivations to change are often prompted once people feel that trouble exists all around them. Lubienski and Lubienski go on to argue that the manufacturing of a perception of trouble is precisely what Milton Friedman had in mind when he suggested that "only a crisis – actual or perceived – produces real change" (Lubienski & Lubienski, 2014, p. 4) which is a disposition towards disaster capitalism as explored by Naomi Klein (2007), embodied by Secretary of Education Arne Duncan's push to replace public schools with charter schools in New Orleans after Hurricane Katrina, and aligns with the broader and decades long manufacturing of a perception of crises in an effort to undermine public education in favor of private options (Berliner & Biddle, 1995; Berliner & Glass, 2014; deMarrais, Brewer, Atkinson, Herron, & Lewis, 2019; Kumashiro, 2012; MacLean, 2017).

When it comes to choosing homeschooling over public education due to the perceived threats that have been manufactured by pro-reform individuals, families, and organizations, the creation and perpetuation of rhetoric that is presented not only as commonsensical but laden with what appear to be statistics reinforces parental concerns about the safety of children and the learning environments at public schools. And this perceived fear is not limited to the United States as concerns about the environment of local schools in Indonesia, as one example, also frequently cite school environments, child safety concerns, special needs of children, and "disagreement" with the government curriculum (Baidi, 2019).

In discussing a newsletter published by Basic Christian Education, Stevens (2001) notes that an article entitled The Basic Educator,

> enumerates a score of problems that apparently are pervasive in American classrooms. The list covers a wide swath: "50 percent of the girls will become pregnant out of wedlock before graduation day. 70 percent of the boys will become sexually active before they leave high school;" children will be "exposed to violence, crime, lack of discipline, and, of course, drugs of every kind;" "Communism and socialism may be presented in the best possible light and capitalism taught as a greed-motivated economic system;" "Many [children] will be exposed to New Age philosophies, Yoga, Transcendental Meditation, witchcraft demonstrations, and Eastern religions." (p. 51)

Tedious as it may be, it is worthwhile to explore each of these typical claims each in turn as parental concern surrounding the environment of public schools is consistently one of the most cited justifications for homeschooling (see Table 2.1).

First, it is important to point out that according to the Centers for Disease Control (CDC) and the U.S. Department of Health & Human Services (HHS), teen pregnancies have been on the decline for decades across the nation (CDC, n.d.; HHS, n.d.). That said, the rate of teen pregnancy is approximately 18.8 per 1,000 women of the ages between 15–19 (CDC, n.d.). Simple mathematical calculation shows that only 1.88% of girls become pregnant prior to (and even a year after) the traditional graduation age of 18. The reality that only 1.88% of girls become pregnant before the age of 20 is a far cry from the fear-mongering statistic suggesting that half of all girls (50%) become pregnant as suggested above. The highest recorded rates of teen pregnancies occurred during the 1950s and 1960s where the rate was 96.3 per 1,000 women or 9.63% of women between the ages of 15–19 (Livingston & Thomas, 2019). That is, teen pregnancy has never in the history of our nation come close to 50% despite the claims of religious fundamentalists. What is interesting, however, is that while religion is used as a justification for avoidance of what is seen as sexual promiscuity and actions that lead to teen pregnancy, teen pregnancy rates are highest in states "whose residents have more conservative religious beliefs" (Jenna, 2009) or colloquially known as the "Bible Belt" due to a avoidance of sex-education, use of and discussions surrounding contraceptives, and the employment of an "abstinence-only" approach to sex (Grady-Pawl, 2017). Additionally, states within the Bible Belt also have rates of teen STDs so high that they are "high enough to be classified as epidemic" (Bushak, 2014).

What is not discernable from the fear-mongering statistic suggesting that 70% of boys become sexually active is how the religious publication defines sexual activity. Despite the unsupported claim that 70% of boys become sexually active before they leave high school, the CDC notes that 44% of teen males have had sex and 42% of females have had sex between the ages of 15–19 (CDC, 2017).

As noted above, sex education is often a topic scorned by many among the religious right. Believing that educating children about sex, safe sex, sexually transmitted diseases, etc. has long been argued as resulting in the encouragement to teenagers to engage in sexual activities. And despite the data explicated above concluding that states that have sex education have better health outcomes than those states who rely on abstinence-only approaches, the myth of a connection between sex education and promiscuity continues to rely on false information. Katherine Stewart (Stewart, 2019) documented how evangelical religious right leaders produce fliers with intentionally misleading information to flame fear about sex education in public schools by using graphic sexual photos that are either not used at all in the curriculum or some of the less graphic ones being labeled as being used at the elementary level when they are, in fact, used at the high school level. Further, Metzel notes that an increase in health-related instruction is likely associated with better long-term health outcomes including, but not limited to, mortality rates (Metzl, 2019). And this makes sense given that states who have either employed an approach of ignoring sex education or using an abstinence-only approach to what is decidedly a healthcare issue, has resulted in higher rates of teen pregnancies and STD transmissions. To put it bluntly, those states where students attend schools with limited (abstinence only) or no exposure to sex education are far more likely to experience teen pregnancy and STDs. As is the case of many religious doctrines, abstinence and virginity are paramount characteristics of what is considered 'holy' and 'pure' for children and young adults pre-marriage. In fact, some fundamentalist Evangelical Christians go as far as holding "purity balls" where a virgin daughter and her father spend the evening dancing while the daughter pledges to remain celibate and "married" to her father until she is actually married (Frank, 2017) as a manifestation of how religious views can shape and inform cultural beliefs.

The claim that attendance at a public school, rather than homeschooling, will expose children to violence, crime, lack of discipline, and drugs has long been a scare tactic. The juxtaposition of public schools as an environment of drugs, alcohol, and violence to the pristine environment of homeschooling has, as explicated in the suggestion above, been a driving fear tactic. In an article published in 2017, we included a notable political cartoon that depicted, on the left side, a downtrodden student with a cigarette in his mouth and hand on a gun above the phrase "public school has so much to offer..." while the right side of the cartoon depicts a smiling boy with his hands posed on a book above the phrase "not like Christian homeschooling!" (Brewer & Lubienski, 2017). The cartoon is meant as tongue-in-cheek sarcasm attempting to illustrate that attendance at a public school will, despite the sarcasm, result in students smoking and using guns while engaging in Christian homeschooling will result in happiness and wholesomeness. Again, playing into the fear mongering narrative that public schools have little to offer other than deviance and amorality.

While there has, seemingly, been an increase in gun-related violence on school campuses in the form of shootings and mass shootings, children are far more likely to have regular exposure to firearms at home. In fact, 1 out of 3 homes in the United States with kids have guns in the home – of which 1.7 million children live in homes where guns are kept unlocked and loaded (Children's Hospital of Philadephia Researach Institute, n.d.). Further, 89% of all children killed as a result of unintentional guns use occurs in the home while children are "playing with a loaded gun in their parent's absence" (Children's Hospital of Philadephia Researach Institute, n.d.). Moreover, gun ownership at home is connected to an increased risk of dying at home as a result of gun-related homicide or suicide (Dahlberg, Ikeda, & Kresnow, 2004; Metzl, 2019). I want to be clear here, I am not suggesting that if A + B = C then C + B should equal A. That is, I am not suggesting that because students are more likely to be injured or killed at home by firearms that the practice of homeschooling would, or does, lead to more firearm deaths. What I am pointing out, however, is the logical fallacy in the argument that it is public schools, as a practice, that brings students into more prevalent contact with guns and, therefore, gun violence as suggested by such cartoons as the one explicated above when children are far more likely to be injured or killed by firearms at home – which happens for all children regardless of whether they are homeschooled or attend public schools. Yet, it does seem to follow that the homeschooling movement – which is largely a movement to deregulate and dismantle public oversight – generally might fall into gun ownership culture. So much so that the HSLDA fought to prevent homeschools from being regulated as gun-free zones (like their public school counterparts) as it represented a "[threat] to home schooling freedoms everywhere" (A2Z Homeschooling, n.d.).

Outside of the perception that public schools expose children to gun violence, there is yet another overlooked reality surrounding violence towards children that many homeschooling advocates ignore: abuse and neglect. The website Homeschooling's Invisible Children offers a searchable national database of instances of child abuse, neglect, and child deaths as a result of abuse and neglect. The site is affiliated with the Coalition for Responsible Home Education (CRHE). A simple search of the CRHE site (CRHE, n.d.-b) for the word "abuse" returns stores with the following phrases or words in the headlines: "verbal and physical abuse was a norm," "homeschooling used to hide abuse," "exploitation," "abuse and torture," "physical abuse and neglect was obvious to me" "children imprisoned" just to name a few. Every year there are national headlines of parents abusing the homeschooling laws to imprison, abuse, exploit, and kill children. Often, these crimes go unnoticed or unknown for long periods of time due to the lack of public oversight in the practice of homeschooling itself but also the lack of having children exposed to adults other than their abusers. Child abuse occurs no matter the type of schooling children are exposed to. But it is the very nature of public engagement through public schools that offers the opportunity for other adults to observe the signs of abuse and work towards ending the abuse. The very nature of homeschooling, while not synonymous with abuse, creates the possibility that those that are abused may go unnoticed until it is too late.

Citing a study published by the Connecticut Office of the Child Advocate, the CRHE reports that a third of all children pulled out of local public schools in order to homeschool in Connecticut did so "after a Department of Child and Family Services (DCF) investigation revealed they were abusing the child(ren)" (Pollack, 2018). Further, "Instead of stopping or slowing down the abuse, the parent(s) instead figured out a way to continue the abuse, and to even escalate the abuse to torture or homicide without being found out: homeschooling. When parents with a prior abuse history pull their children out of school to 'homeschool' them, this needs to be understood as an escalation and cover up of their criminal activity" (Pollack, 2018). The Homeschooling's Invisible Children database operated by CRHE contends that,

> preliminary research suggests that homeschooled children are at a greater risk of dying from child abuse than are traditionally schooled children. This preliminary finding is based on an analysis of the cases in

> our Homeschooling's Invisible Children (HIC) database and on national government reports on child maltreatment. When we compare the rate of child abuse fatalities among homeschooled families to the rate of child abuse fatalities overall, we see a higher rate of death due to abuse or neglect among homeschooled students than we do among children of the same age overall. (Children, n.d.)

This reality is not difficult to understand given that cases of abuse are often uncovered by public school teachers and counselors who come in contact with students on a daily basis. As state mandated reporters, suspicion of abuse or neglect are reported to the proper authorities within 24 hours. Students who are homeschooled are more likely to not come into contact with adults outside of family members or with individuals who have a legal mandate to report suspicious activity or signs of abuse that can lead to short or long term trauma and/or death. And, as noted in Chapter 1, the national shuttering of public schools for temporary schooling-at-home measures in response to the COVID-19 pandemic saw a dramatic decrease in the number of abuse cases being reported (Prabhu, 2020). This raises some significant questions about how to regulate the normal traditional practice of homeschooling to ensure that abuse and neglect are not going unnoticed. To that end, following the unreported death of a homeschooled child, the Coalition for Responsible Home Education has advocated for a change to Florida law to include a required in-person check-in with the homeschooling family from a certified teacher each school year (Rozyla, 2015).

Turning back to the other claims above that include claims that "Communism and socialism may be presented in the best possible light and capitalism taught as a greed-motivated economic system;" finds that this claim is not exclusive to the homeschooling community. Indeed, as the Red Scare led to McCarthyism in the 1950s, teachers and public schools became a target for their supposedly anti-American, anti-Capitalism, pro-Communism stance. Teachers were required to sign loyalty pledges denouncing communism out of threat of losing their jobs (Goldstein, 2014). But paranoia about public schools promoting socialism and communism over capitalism did not end with the end of McCarthyism. Organizations such as TurningPoint USA with close ties to the Trump administration have long pushed the claim that K-12 schools and college campuses are a breeding ground for communism and socialism in addition to the denigration of capitalism. One of the most notable educational pamphlets published by TPUSA is its "How to Debate Your Teacher (and Win!): Empowering Students to Have the Confidence to Defend their Beliefs in Classrooms and Universities." The opening lines argue that, "Today, teachers and professors all across the country are training young minds to believe that capitalism is immoral. It's up to YOU to stand up for what you believe in" (Turning Point USA, 2015a, foreword ). In all, the piece is offered without substantiation and relies heavily on emotional appeal and fear-mongering. Accordingly,

> This booklet is designed to empower students to fight back against this progressive aggression in our schools. Turning Point USA has outlined a blueprint to deter the typical strategies used by teachers and professors; we have also provided tips to swing the narrative away from indoctrination toward a balanced classroom environment. Throughout this booklet we highlight real life success stories of students who stood up to their teachers and successfully prevented outward anti free enterprise aggression from occurring in their classrooms. We show you that it is possible to fight back and enlighten your fellow classmates to the truth about history, civics, and economics. (Turning Point USA, 2015a, foreword)

Arguing that public school K-12 teachers and college professors are radical leftists, TPUSA like so many other organizations that center fear mongering as a political strategy, argue that "everybody has that one crazy liberal professor that drives you absolutely insane. Whether they obsess over wealth distribution, bash capitalism, or try to paint the free market as the most awful economic system to ever exist, they are teaching liberalism rather than fact" (Turning Point USA, 2015a, p. 1). Contrary to avoiding the public sphere by way of homeschooling, for example, TPUSA hopes its followers attack, head on, the very things that drive some families away from public schools and public universities in favor of homeschooling and/or private education. It is worth noting that TPUSA is part of a growing network of conservative and neoconservative organizations that share ties with the school reform and school privatization agenda (Brewer & Swain, 2020) including organizations such as Reason that often pushes false narratives about homeschooling (Tuccille, 2019).

Further, claims that capitalism is taught as a "greed-motivated economic system" in schools represents a misdirection or misunderstanding of the tenets of capitalism that quite literally center on self-interested individualism. Of the notable literature often cited by conservatives and republicans in their defense of capitalism and free-markets is the seminal work *Atlas Shrugged* by Ayn Rand (1957/1999) where individual self-interest and greed improve the lives of the individual and, in turn, society. If everyone is able to focus on bettering their own lives, sans influence and the burdens of government and collective society, then the individualism described in Rand's work (or, greed) is the driving factor in societal improvement.

## 2 A Brief History of Teacher Preparation

Given the myriad early forms of schooling in the U.S., there was not much in the way of formalized teacher preparation or a process of teacher certification. As most early schools – overseen by local communities and towns – focused primarily on teaching the Bible (Fraser, 2014; Urban & Wagoner, 2009), individuals who were seen to be moral, upstanding, and who possessed knowledge of the Bible were hired to teach. The formal requirements for maintaining a job as a teacher included, in some instances, less attention on being a 'good teacher' and more on being a 'good person' as evidenced by their being prohibited from riding in cars with men other than a father or brother and not being allowed to spend time in downtown ice-cream shops.

Among the most notable early forms of a more formalized preparation for teachers can be found in Catharine Beecher's Hartford Female Seminary where she sought to train women for work as teachers. And while Beecher's ideology was one that both celebrated the traditional role of woman-at-home, she also forged new understandings about the role of women outside of the home – dominantly as school teachers (Urban & Wagoner, 2009) – as she advocated for the United States to open the types of "normal" schools that trained teachers in the same way that France and Prussia (Prussia's form of schooling becoming the model upon which U.S. schools ultimately were modeled after) trained teachers (Beecher, 1835). Normal schools would, in time, become the modern colleges of education that oversaw teacher preparation. To this day, traditional colleges of education and "traditionally certified teachers" are the mainstay of teacher preparation in the U.S. And while every college of education differs in its approach, they have certainly evolved from Beecher's regulations and oversight that was grounded in her theology, to oversight from the Council for the Accreditation of Educator Preparation (CAEP) that now regulates almost all traditional forms of teacher preparation. CAEP is a recent consolidation of the National Council for the Accreditation of Teacher Education (NCATE) that began in 1954 with the goal of "rais[ing] the quality of preparation [of teachers]" and the Teacher Education Accreditation Council (TEAC) founded in 1997 to ensure evidence-based qualifications (Council for the Accreditation of Educator Preparation, n.d.).

Juxtaposed to the traditionally certified teacher and colleges of education are those teachers who enter the profession by way of an alternative certification program/organization that circumvents the years of coursework, practicum experience, and in many cases, the pedagogical tenants of teacher preparation associated with colleges of education. The term "alternative" in the phrase alternative teacher preparation aptly situates teacher preparation within the recent historical context of housing teacher preparation within colleges of education. On the face of it, alternative certification programs operate under the auspices of: (1) injecting competition into the "monopoly" of teacher preparation historically held by state universities; and/or (2) under the assertion and façade that teacher preparation can be expedited and that extensive training in both methodology and practicum practice (e.g., student teaching) is thus not a necessary component of sufficient teacher preparation. Additionally, alternative certification processes and organizations have received increasing support for expansion given the purported difficulty of staffing teachers in "hard-to-staff" schools – often urban schools that serve predominately non-White and non-affluent students. The combination of those assumptions work to reify the existence of alternative certification programs as a necessity to combat burdensome government oversight (like CAEP) and expenses at the state level (e.g., funding for colleges of education) in addition to offering individuals who aspire to be teachers a faster – and assuredly cheaper – entry into the field while seemingly serving as the best solution to a problem that traditional colleges of education have not been able to solve. However, as noted by some (Roth & Swail, 2000), since the advent of teacher colleges (e.g., traditional certification) did not occur until the late nineteenth and early twentieth century, that alternative certification routes (in this definition, alternative meaning less formalized as is now the case of the traditional route) were actually the basis of teacher credentialing. That is, since local communities were responsible for hiring teachers and there existed no colleges of education – or normal schools at the time – the credentialing process was not formalized and was entirely up to local leaders to determine what constituted a 'qualified' teacher. Again, that determination was up to the discretion of community leaders and their evaluation of an individual's grasp on the Bible and other moral expectations.

Alternative certification programs have taken on many shapes and sizes. The most notable of nation-wide programs include Teach For America (TFA), the New Teacher Project (TNTP), and the Relay Graduate School of Education (formerly known as "Teacher U"). There are also city-specific programs like the New York City Teaching Fellows in addition to state-specific programs for alternative licensing. However, the latter state-based licensing programs tend to not recruit candidates; rather, they provide coursework often in partnership with a local university's college of education for individuals who are seeking employment as a teacher but do not have a traditional background in education. TNTP was founded in 1997 by TFA alumna Michelle Rhee and functions in similar ways to that of TFA. Though, an important branching off specific to TNTP has been the organization's production of original research that has argued that teacher unions are one of the main obstacles to education reform (Levin, Mulhern, & Schunck, 2005). Recently TNTP produced a study that concluded that current forms of teacher professional development are inadequate and that professional development should be more specific towards helping teachers increase metrics (e.g., test scores) (The New Teacher Project, 2015). TNTP founder Rhee became the Chancellor of D.C. Public Schools in 2007 and resigned in 2010 following an election cycle and accusations of cheating. Following her resignation, Rhee established Students First, a lobbying organization that publishes state-based grading scale each year in addition to providing political and financial support for anti-union activities. With the help of Students Matter (an organization that is supported by Rhee and Students First), the high profile anti-teacher union case of *Vegara v California* made national headlines as the decision of the Court found that teacher tenure laws were unconstitutional (Students Matter, 2014; "Vergara v. California," 2014).

Yet, as will be explored below, the phenomenon and practice of homeschooling eschews all parameters of a traditional or professional sense of what it means to be trained sufficiently to teach children.

## 3    Who Is Capable of Teaching at Home?

Certainly one of the most notable components of homeschooling is that a parent (or some combination of adults) is responsible for teaching one, and in many cases more than one, student at home. As a result, questions surrounding the qualifications of those who teach are a necessary component of the homeschooling discussion and debate. Again, this question aligns with the overarching consideration of the role, function, and limits of parental sovereignty and notions of the role and authority of the state to provide formal education. Weaving throughout considerations of who can, should, and ought to be allowed to teach (in any form of schooling whether it be public, private, or homeschooling) is the notion and understanding of expertise. Generally speaking, expertise comes with a significant level of regulation on who enters into a specific field of knowledge and practice. Parents naturally possess the right of parental sovereignty as a natural function of being a parent. This authority generally remains unquestioned and unchallenged apart from a violation of societal norms surrounding agreed upon limits of that sovereignty (e.g., neglect and abuse) where the state's responsibility and authority overrides parental sovereignty. While parents are the natural teachers of their children at home in terms of socialization, family culture, family beliefs, and oversee early physical development (e.g., crawling, walking, and speaking), the practice of homeschooling extends the understanding and boundaries of parental sovereignty to define parents as being qualified to provide and deliver educational curriculum. Said more plainly, some homeschooling advocates suggest that because a parent is the one who teaches a child how to tie her shoe, the parent is the natural-best person to teach the child organic chemistry (Bryant, 2020). What is interesting here is that crawling, walking, and speaking are often held up as examples of early educative lessons taught to children by their parents. And while it is true that parents assist children with these things, crawling and walking would occur naturally and speaking is developed through mimicking, listening, and practicing. Keeping in mind that notions of proper syntax are concepts created by professionals and many homeschooling parents themselves, learned proper grammar and speaking syntax from public schools and the professional teachers who staff them.

With that in mind, I want to point out here that I am, myself, a parent twice over. At the time of this writing, my daughter was 5, nearly 6, and my son was 4. My wife, their mother, and I did our best and aim to continue in those efforts that aid and assist our children in their natural and healthy development. We installed rubber foam around the raised fireplace hearth when our son started walking (we did not have this feature in the house we lived in when our daughter was learning to walk) so as to help prevent injuries as he did stumble and fall, as all children do when they learn to walk. At times, we chose to take our children outside so that they could learn to walk on more uneven surfaces such as the sidewalk that went around the circumference of our neighborhood block. The problem with walking on sidewalks – and later running on them as toddlers and kindergartners – is that falls often result in skinned knees. As caring parents, we showed our children how to put on bandages (often with whimsical cartoon characters that, apparently, helped soothe the pain) that would aid in the slowing of bleeding and prevention of infection. While she may not want to admit it – especially through the tears of a contemporary need for a bandage on a skinned knee – I'm quite sure that my daughter can adequately open and position a bandage on a scraped knee. With no doubt, this is something that we taught her as her parents and, in a way, as her educators. However, it would be beyond any reasonable explanation to suggest that either of us as parents are qualified, equipped, or adequately prepared to tend to a broken bone as a result of a harder fall. In fact, it would likely be reasonable to suggest that a claim that I, by virtue of being the parent, am qualified or more qualified than a medical professional to reset a bone, cast a leg, schedule and provide antibiotics if the break of the bone penetrates the surface of the skin would be akin to parental malfeasance or negligence. My teaching of how to apply a bandage is not sufficient or adequate experience necessary to address anything more medically serious than a minor scrape on a knee. It is not enough to know how to suture a larger wound. My knowledge and experience of putting antiseptic creams on a scratch is not sufficient or adequate experience to teach my child about biology or chemistry – even with the added aid of YouTube videos or mail-order curriculum. This is telling of how homeschooling families interpret the importance, profession, and rigor of education. That is, if they can teach small and early curriculum content to their children, then they are well suited to teach the more rigorous concepts and content later on. Not only is it problematic to claim that parents are well equipped or prepared to teach early childhood curriculum, but it is overtly clear that claims of qualifications to teach advanced curriculum are misguided.

In comparison, educator authority – as an extension of the state's authority – is gained through a credentialing and legal process whereby individuals receive rigorous training that results in a license to teach. Such a credential conveys a level of expertise of subject matter, child development, pedagogy, and curriculum development. In short, homeschooling parents posit that the nature of being a parent provides the extended rationale for educating whereas the broader society posits that authority to teach must first be established by traditional training, credentialing, licensing, and broader understandings of entering a profession. Believing that parents are capable of teaching by nature of being a parent holds that authority and ability to teach curriculum is a natural byproduct of parenthood rather than earned expertise. Yet, this tension is not limited to questions of authority as many "homeschoolers are also wary of state intrusion into family life and generally are skeptical of the ability of bureaucracies and 'experts' to meet the task of child rearing" This dichotomy undermines traditional understandings of expertise and a profession as both are surrounded by specialized knowledge held by "people who have mastered particular skills or bodies of knowledge and who practice those skills or use that knowledge as their main occupation in life" (Nichols, 2017, p. 29) being a prerequisite for qualification as opposed to qualification by individual fiat.

Central to the belief that anyone can teach and the American adage of "those who can, do and those who can't, teach" is the assumption that teaching and education is not in and of itself a profession, rather, a technocratic skill that can be easily learned or exist without intensive and specific training. Howsam et al. (1976, pp. 15–16) provide a useful overview of the characteristics of a profession as:

1.  Professions are occupationally related social institutions established and maintained as a means of providing essential services to the individual and the society;

2. Each profession is concerned with an identified area of need or function (e.g., maintenance of physical and emotional health, preservation of rights and freedom, enhancing the opportunity to learn);

3. The profession collectively, and the professional individually, possesses a body of knowledge and a repertoire of behaviors and skills (professional culture) needed in the practice of the profession; such knowledge, behavior, and skills normally are not possessed by the nonprofessional;

4. The members of the profession are involved in decision making in the service of the client, the decisions being made in accordance with the most valid knowledge available, against a background of principals and theories, and within the context of possible impact on other related conditions or decisions;

5. The profession is based on one or more undergirding disciplines from which it draws basic insights and upon which it builds its own applied knowledge and skills

6. The profession is organized into one or more professional associations which, within broad limits of social accountability, are granted autonomy in control of the actual work of the profession and the conditions which surround it (admissions, educational standards, examination and licensing, career line, ethical and performance standards, professional discipline).

7. The profession has agreed-upon performance standards for admission to the profession and for continuance within it

8. Preparation for and induction to the profession is provided through a protracted preparation program, usually in a professional school on a college or university campus;

9. There is a high level of public trust and confidence in the profession and in individual practitioners, based upon the profession's demonstrated capacity to provide service markedly beyond that which would otherwise be available;

10. Individual practitioners are characterized by a strong service motivation and lifetime commitment to competence;

11. Authority to practice in any individual case derives from the client or the employing organization; accountability for the competence of professional practice within the particular case is to the profession itself;

12. There is relative freedom from direct on-the-job supervision and from direct public evaluation of the individual practitioner. The professional accepts responsibility in the name of his or her profession and is accountable through his or her profession to the society.

While the profession of teaching is not without its contemporary barriers to realizing, in full, the above characteristics of a profession (Brewer & Cody, 2014; Goldstein, 2014; Ravitch, 2010, 2013)

> Every society has certain functions to be performed if life within it is to be sustained and if the quality of life is to be maintained or improved. Societies differ, however, in the way they organize to provide for performance of these functions. Simple societies diffuse the functions over populations. Complex societies, on the other hand, create work specialization and invent institutions and organizations to facilitate delivery and improvement of services. (Howsam et al., 1976, p. 14)

They go on to suggest that complex modern societies have necessitated the creation of five occupational categories: (1) professional; (2) semiprofessional; (3) paraprofessional; (4) skilled; and (5) unskilled trade.

> Each of these represents service to others, made necessary by the reality that few if any people possess the knowledge and skills needed or the inclination to be self-sufficient in meeting their own needs. Thus, the difference between levels of occupations is not in the element of service, but in the nature of the service. Some needs are so fundamental that failure to meet them seriously interferes with the quality of life or with life itself. Professions customarily involve this kind of service. (Howsam et al., 1976, p. 14)

With this understanding in mind, we must ask ourselves if we consider the education and socialization of future generations of our society as fundamentally connected to a continued quality of life and the perpetuation of life itself. In a traditional sense, Horace Mann and, to a lesser extent, Thomas Jefferson understood that free and public education, compulsory up to a certain age, was the fundamental cornerstone to the survival of our nation and democracy. Thus, if we consider schooling and education as the bedrock of our democracy in our complex society, the perspective of Howsam et al. would require that education be an enterprise led by professionals and not treated as either a characteristic of a simple society or an endeavor not associated with the perpetuation of a society's quality of life – or the life of the society itself. In understanding the need for professional educators, the faith and trust in the ability to educate is not situated with an individual but rather within the broader institution of education that is "responsible for insuring that service to the client is competent within the limits of the existing art or science...the profession is the source of that confidence and assurance" (Howsam et al., 1976, p. 15).

There are 29 states that require a parent provide an annual notice that their child(ren) will be homeschooled for the upcoming school year – a constant documentation process in response to national compulsory schooling laws while there are ten states that require only a one-time notice and 11 states that require no notice be given (CRHE, n.d.-a).

The majority of states do not require a homeschooling parent to have, themselves, any formal level of education prior to assuming the role of educator within the home (Huseman, 2015). That is, there is no requirement of either a high school diploma or college degree. In short, a homeschooling parent could, themselves, have completed no more than the 5th grade, for example, and charge themselves with teaching K-12 (including advanced subjects experienced in high school). Those 38 states are:

| | | |
|---|---|---|
| – Alabama | – Kentucky | – New Jersey |
| – Alaska | – Louisiana | – New York |
| – Arizona | – Maine | – Oklahoma |
| – Arkansas | – Maryland | – Oregon |
| – Colorado | – Massachusetts | – Rhode Island |
| – Connecticut | – Michigan | – South Carolina |
| – Delaware | – Minnesota | – Tennessee |
| – Florida | – Mississippi | – Texas |
| – Hawaii | – Missouri | – Utah |
| – Idaho | – Montana | – Vermont |
| – Illinois | – Nebraska | – Wisconsin |
| – Indiana | – Nevada | – Wyoming |
| – Iowa | – New Hampshire | |

And there are 2 states (California and Kansas) that require a homeschooling parent be able to show that they are "capable" of teaching yet, as ProPublica points out, there are no laws within those states as to qualify what constitutes capability and "officials are not allowed to exercise discretion" (Huseman, 2015).

There are 9 states that only require that a homeschooling parent hold a high school diploma, yet, 4 of those states (District of Columba, Ohio, North Dakota, and Virginia), allow that requirement to be waived though evidence that a parent can prove their ability to teach or through a temporary monitoring of some form before the requirement is waived (Huseman, 2015). Those states requiring only a high school diploma are:

- District of Columbia
- Georgia
- New Mexico
- North Carolina
- North Dakota
- Ohio
- Pennsylvania
- South Dakota
- Virginia

The determination on whether or not a parent is educationally qualified to teach in West Virginia is left to the discretion of a local superintendent. Parents wishing to be the lead educator in the lives of their child(ren) in Washington must satisfy one of four requirements: (1) be supervised by a certified person; (2) achieve a minimum number of college credits (e.g., hold a high school diploma and have completed "some" college); (3) have taken a course in how to homeschool; or, (4) been deemed qualified by their local school board (Huseman, 2015). So, in short, the most rigorous educational attainment standards for a parent to be the primary/lead educator in the lives of children by way of a homeschool is having an educational experience no greater than what they may themselves be teaching. This reality stands in stark contrast to what is actually a rigorous training and credentialing process that public school teachers undergo prior to being charged with leading the educational experiences, learning, and assessments of students. Educators teaching in public K-12 systems must at least have a bachelor's degree from an accredited university as, generally speaking, the standard practice in regulated education is that an educator must hold one degree higher than the level in which she is teaching with the notable exception of the doctoral level as it is a terminal degree:

| Teaching level | Required degree level |
| --- | --- |
| K-12 | Bachelor's |
| Bachelor's | Masters |
| Masters | Doctorate |

More to the point, the requirements to teach as an educator in a public K-12 school require that, prior to being hired, a teaching candidate complete the course of study through a college of education. In addition to detailed and extensive content-area course training, a teaching candidate will, through their traditional training, receive and complete training in a myriad of pedagogical and developmental courses that include:

- Critical and Contemporary Issues in Education (history of education, educational policy, etc.)
- Sociocultural Diversity
- Educational Psychology (how students learn, develop, learning theories, assessment theories, etc.)
- Teaching Reading in a Content Area
- Curriculum & Pedagogy
- Classroom Data Analysis
- Educational Assessment
- Coursework on Teaching students with Exceptionalities
- Classroom Management
- Content-specific Methods coursework

Further, public school teacher candidates must also complete hundreds of hours of observations, mini-lessons, and either a half-year or full-year student internship where the candidate gradually takes over classroom responsibilities under the supervision of a fully licensed veteran teacher. This entire practicum experience is assessed by not only the local educators within the school where the student teaching experience is occurring but also under the supervision of a university-based professor of education and ultimately assessed in many states using the edTPA educator assessment and some state-level credentialing exam (e.g., the Praxis exam or other varied state versions of the test). While assessment instruments such as edTPA are wholly not without their problems (Carter & Lochte, 2017; Kumashiro, 2015; Mathis, 2013; Whitaker & Burns, 2019), the approach marks a stark difference in accountability when approving individuals with the steep task of educating the next generation.

Yet, homeschooling does not interpret education as a profession and, simultaneously, understands the act of teaching as an endeavor that does not require extensive training prior to taking on the responsibility of teaching. At a session designed for parents who were considering or in the early stages of beginning to homeschool at the Southeast Homeschooling Expo, one of the opening speakers explored the likelihood that those in the room would certainly encounter push-back and objections to their decision to homeschool by both their family and friends. The speaker noted that among the top objections that they would encounter are people questioning their ability to provide an education for children – particularly given that there are not stringent educational or credentialing requirements. Further, the speaker noted that there would be times where the parent who is homeschooling may very well question their own ability and qualifications to be the sole educator for their children. To both these external and internal objections, the speaker stated that, "when people ask you what makes you qualified to teach your children [algebra, chemistry, reading, history, etc.], tell them that you're the most qualified person on the planet because you gave birth to them." Again, this disposition towards understanding teaching not as a profession but as something that can be done without training and, in this case, is best done as a result of birthing, draws back into focus the overarching disdain for expertise within the homeschooling community. Along the lines explored at the opening of this chapter related to the argument that a parent, by fiat of being a parent, is the most suited to teach their children, homeschooling advocates push this logic often. A notable homeschool blogger claims that, "Rest assured that, as a parent, you are the best teacher your children could have. No one knows your children better than you" (Linsenbach, 2010, p. 18). Imagine, for a moment, that the word "teacher" were replaced in the sentence above and whether or not the rationale or justification would still stand. For example, if "teacher" were replaced with, say, "doctor," or "lawyer," or "nutritionist," etc., the sentence would seemingly fall apart under the justification that because one is a parent, one is qualified. Again, similar to the claims mentioned above about a natural qualification due to birthing a child, Linsenbach suggests that, "You might be concerned that you 'don't know how to teach.' But you have already been and continue to be your child's teacher. You are the one who cared for your child as a baby, and you are the one who taught your baby to walk, to talk, to eat the right foods, to cross a street safely, to treat others kindly, and much more" (Linsenbach, 2010, pp. 18–19). Linsenbach doubles down on many of these claims that are worth including at length here:

> Yes, you can homeschool your child! You needn't be a professional teacher to educate your child at home. Children are natural learners, and parents are natural teachers. You've seen your child learn and grow with your guidance and love since the day your son or daughter was born. Homeschooling is similar to parenting your child and just as rewarding! (Linsenbach, 2010, p. 15)

> From the earliest days, a child's education took place inside the home. Children learned from parents, from a large extended family, and from everyday life. They learned to read books on their own or from older siblings. They practiced their alphabet, penmanship, and math problems on slate with a slate pencil. Families made sure their children learned important life skills; reading, writing, and math skills; and socialization skills. They taught their children morals and values, proper manners and etiquette, how to get along with others, and how to respect their elders. (Linsenbach, 2010, p. 16)

As the Industrial Revolution swept the country, school transportation improved and so did attendance at public schools. However, in the 1960s and 1970s, some families, disappointed with the public school system, began teaching their children at home. Early homeschool pioneers and advocates broke new ground in the homeschool territory. Family-centered education began moving to the forefront of society again. (Linsenbach, 2010, p. 17)

What is not mentioned here, however, is that the 1960s and 1970s were an era of racial integration within public schools and, as Linsenbach eludes to, school transportation using busses were employed under bussing policies specifically designed to help integrate schools – particularly in areas that were hesitant to federal integration rulings and laws. While there are little overt nods towards choosing to homeschool out of racist intent, many of the foundational policies supporting school choice (e.g., homeschooling expansion, school vouchers, and charter schools) have included a desire to avoid racial integration (Brewer & Potterton, 2020; MacLean, 2017).

Much of the central theme with the belief that a parent is the best teacher for their child because they know their children better than any other adult seems to be a persistent and common theme in other areas of life normally understood to be best served by professionals rather than novices. For example, the past decade has seen a massive increase in the anti-vaccine movement for a myriad of reasons. Chiefly among them is the false-belief that vaccines cause autism. That is, many parents believe that there is a causal relationship between vaccines (specifically the Measles, Mumps, and Rubella – or MMR vaccine) and the onset/manifestation of autism. Failing to understand that correlation does not imply causation, the myth of the link between vaccinations and autism became popularized by a, now redacted, peer-reviewed study published in the top medical journal *The Lancet*. While the lead author of the study has since lost his medical license and the study has been thoroughly debunked by subsequent studies, the damage inflicted remains. And while the vast majority of American citizens do not read peer-reviewed articles (namely because they are behind paywalls and employ a significant level of professional jargon), the myth of a link between vaccines and autism has been promoted and sustained by a slew of celebrities like Jenny McCarthy and Jim Carrey and if there is anything to be said about American culture, the typical American is infatuated by celebrity. And while not all anti-vax parents arrive at such a disposition as a direct result of celebrity influence, it seems that most arrive at such conclusions by way of conducting internet "research." While the internet has been a boon for information and even fostering the rise of democracies as was the case of the Arab Spring, the internet is equally full of misinformation that often reinforces echo chambers and confirmation biases across every conceivable topic of consideration – vaccines, politics, religion, and homeschooling. A random sampling of the comment sections on pseudo-medical blogs or social media like Facebook and Twitter will likely return dozens of comments of defensive anti-vaxxers (as they are known) either suggesting on the front end that they have "done their research" and/or will attempt to end a discussion with some iteration of, "well, you just need to do your own research like I did." Internet "research," again, often results in the generation of echo chambers and biases but also erodes at the notion of expertise. Additionally, the connotation of "research" and the access of information (particularly the ability to access information that results in confirmation bias) establishes the belief that any and all information is of equal value. As a result, it is often the case that people feel empowered to argue with experts – say, a physician or a representative of the Centers for Disease Control and Prevention – in a way that elevates a degree from the "University of Google" with that of actual expert knowledge. In fact, "there is no way to enlighten people who believe they've gained a decade's worth of knowledge because they've spent a morning with a search engine. Few words in a discussion with a lay-person can make an expert's heart sink like hearing 'I've done some research'" (Nichols, 2017, p. 120). As Nichols goes on to suggest, "Americans now think of democracy as a state of actual equality, in which every opinion is as good as any other on almost any subject under the sun" (Nichols, 2017, p. 232).

This false sense of expertise and possession of "knowledge" that gives the façade of expert knowledge is part-and-parcel of the landscape that reinforces the belief that a biological parent who has "found some online resources" is just as qualified, if not more qualified, than a professional educator who has completed a rigorous course of study and credentialing process.

My point here is not to draw parallels to what are seemingly disparate forms of anti-intellectualism, anti-expertise, or anti-professionalism, in an attempt to make one group guilty by association. However, the point here is that vaccinations and the growing trend of parents to assert parental sovereignty and online "research" over the qualifications of actual experts and what is to be understood as a societal commitment to maintaining itself. Further, there is an overt connection between the homeschooling movement and the anti-vaccine movement as the HSLDA specifically rates states on their friendliness to homeschoolers with a category on whether or not the state still requires children to be vaccinated (HSLDA, n.d.; Huseman, 2015). Thus, the deregulation of schooling (by way of homeschooling) and the deregulation of vaccinations (allowing parents to opt-out either as public school attendees or, in this case, homeschoolers) go hand-in-hand with what can be best understood as a belief that parents are the most suitable, knowledgeable, and best providers of education and medical intervention in the lives of their children. Some of this, it would seem, stems from the broader anti-intellectual movement but it also stems from a political philosophy more closely aligned with libertarianism and notions of rugged individualism. In fact, Bethany Mandel, a homeschooling parent, penned an Op-Ed in the New York Times pointing out that the anti-vax movement and the homeschooling movement are aligned as a "go-against-the-grain attitude."

Yet, while Mandel makes a strong argument for the connections between the anti-vax movement and homeschooling, she failed to see the irony of wanting to push back against the anti-professionalism of the anti-vax environment within the anti-professionalism of the homeschooling movement which, in the same column, lauded. On the one hand, Mandel praises medical expertise, the importance of herd immunity, and the ability of the State to step in and act on behalf of the larger society by superseding parental sovereignty. What is not acknowledged in Mandel's arguments, and others like it, is that as society has become more complex and thus warranted a professional approach to education – as discussed above – the maintenance of a complex society demands that we establish educational professionals, a herd-immunity when it comes to knowledge and education, and ultimately the ability of the State (the formal society) to supersede notions of parental sovereignty. That is, following the metaphor of how we understand herd-immunity as a mechanism through which immunity among a majority of the population naturally protects not only itself but it protects the spread of disease by not providing willful hosts – thus not only protecting the most vulnerable individuals in the herd but the herd as a whole. It seems to follow that notions of compulsory public education as espoused by Mann and Jefferson sought to provide the same level of herd-immunity when it came to facts, knowledge, training, and skills. For a society to survive a preventable outbreak of a communicable disease, herd-immunity is a necessary component. Equally, for society to survive communicable ignorance (both in the sense of preventing the spread of true knowledge as well as the suppression of false myths – say, that vaccines cause autism), there must be a standard inoculation provided to society if it is to survive itself. Otherwise, when education is approached as everyone for themselves, not only does actual truth become siloed in a bubble, it creates the capacity for rumor, fear, and conspiracy to roam freely (think, women as witches during the Salem witch trials) that results in rule by paranoia.

In continuing with the parallel of vaccinations, if you will permit, it may be of use to think about the dosage and schedule of dosage as a metaphor for how education can serve as the inoculation against society's downfall. In the same way that many vaccines are scheduled to be delivered in small doses over time, much of our general approach to school curriculum is done in the same manner. And while there is much to be discussed about some of the downfalls of piecemeal instruction – notably a discussion beyond the scope of this work – it is worthwhile to compare and contrast the scope and sequence of content exposure between a typical traditional public school and what is recommended for homeschooling instruction. A speaker at the Southeast Homeschool Expo suggested that, "students K-6 should only be spending 30–60 minutes per day doing 'school' but that's more than what they get in public schools because teachers have to spend most of their time breaking up fights and settling students down" (Henn, 2019). Similarly, Linsenbach suggests that:

> The actual time required to focus on core skills (language arts, reading, social studies, math, and science) can be broken down per age group as follows:
> – Preschool and Kindergarten: 30 to 60 minutes per day
> – Elementary-school ages: 60 to 90 minutes per day
> – Middle-school ages: 1.5 to 3 hours per day
> – High-school ages: 2 to 4 hours per day. (Linsenbach, 2010, p. 23)

By comparison, public school schedules generally practice the following:
– Preschool and kindergarten: Academic content typically focuses on reading and writing and other soft skills such as letter recognition, calendar literacy, that exceeds 30–60 minutes per day while a significant portion is dedicated to structured and unstructured play and socialization.
– Elementary-school ages: Skews heavily towards reading, writing, and mathematics and can range from 1.5 and 2 hours each day in reading and writing and another 1.5 hours in math with a ranging amount of time dedicated to other content subjects such as social studies, science, and the arts while providing structured and unstructured opportunities for socialization.
– Middle-school ages: 55–65 minutes per content/subject, generally totaling 6 hours per day spent in content-knowledge courses with additional time spent in extracurricular and social activities.
– High-school ages: 55–65 minutes per content/subject, generally totaling 6 hours per day spent in content-knowledge courses with additional time spent in extracurricular and social activities.

Assuming that children attending public schools are in a learning environment for 7 hours per day for a standard school year of 180 days, students attending public schools from Kindergarten to 12th grade would amass 1,260 hours per school year or 16,380 over the duration of 13 years of school. Following the suggested time for homeschooling as explicated above, a student homeschooled from Kindergarten to 12th grade would amass between 3,240 and 6,030 across the same 13 years. On the conservative end, that would mean that a homeschooled student spends only 20% of the time that a public school student does focused on academic work. To be sure, not every single moment of every single minute in a public school academic classroom is focused (intentionally or not) on learning but so too is it likely that budgeted time at home for academic work can be distracted by the student or external forces.

Academic time aside, homeschooling families often see their "incentive, apparently, [as] a mix of religious conviction and a suspicion that the public schools were not adequately doing their job" (Stevens, 2001, p. 3) or that the needs of children who are homeschooled are "too distinctive to be handed over to strangers" (Stevens, 2001, p. 4). No matter the rationale or justification (or combination of them), the fundamental presupposition of homeschooling is that public schools not sufficient educative environments or represent a negative to be avoided.

In his seminal text, Mitchell Stevens documents that, "Homeschoolers also are wary of state intrusion into family life and generally are skeptical of the ability of bureaucracies and 'experts' to meet the task of child rearing" (Stevens, 2001, p. 5). Additionally, Stevens (2001) notes that,

> Schools are bad because they do not treat children as individuals. Children have problems in school because schools do not serve their individual needs. Schools are like factories, but children are not like machines. Children are unique, but schools do not honor that uniqueness. These contrasts, repeated by many speakers in many kinds of texts and read by home schoolers time and again, forge a view of children as unique persons that conventional schools can never adequately serve. Once inside this literature, parents are encouraged by its litany of claims to lend the uniqueness of their children great importance. Distinctiveness is rendered too significant and too fragile to be entrusted to others. (p. 43)

In other ways, the rise of homeschooling can, perhaps, be understood as a response to the increasing burden placed on students in public schools that have exchanged education for schooling. That is, as high-stakes testing accountability has decidedly demoralized the education climate in schools in its attempt to standardize learning and outcomes, alternative approaches to education that embrace, at its core, a more humanizing disposition towards children is understandable.

The issue, however, is that while the abandonment of the public sphere in favor of the individual child (even as a good faith exercise of what is best for the humanity of children) is a form of school choice that is explicitly not available to all students. Given the vast amount of financial resources it often requires to homeschool (namely the forgoing of a parental salary so that a parent can remain home with the children), the relatively more affluent families that are able to opt-out of what they see as a dehumanizing public school process create, by default, a concentration of less fortunate students in the public school who are not able to provide the means of an individualized education at home. The very nature of public education and common schools was devised explicitly because the majority of children in the United States could not afford private home tutors (Urban & Wagoner, 2009). To the ends that it is correct to understand the dehumanizing tendencies of public schools as a justification for seceding away from the public sphere, the practice exacerbates and highlights the growing financial disparities in American society and likely reinforces some of the more negative experiences within public schools as families who have a considerable amount of social and cultural capital could otherwise leverage to improve public schools rather than abandoning them all together. In their abandonment of public education to focus on the individualistic needs of their own children, communities suffer the long-term impacts of a public school system that is devoid of involvement from families that could help improve the schools and, as a result, ensure the short and long term efficacy of their own community and the nation with an understanding of the role that public education plays at both the local and national level.

Historically, the United States economy afforded the opportunity for White mothers to be stay-at-home parents. Our pop culture artifacts of television shows, movies, and songs often present the mother as homemaker in shows such as *Leave it to Beaver* and *Mad Men*. And while this single-parent income of the nostalgic 50s was largely not an opportunity enjoyed by non-White families – and to some extent, not actually as pervasive as nostalgic myths might have us believe (Coontz, 1992) – the changing economic conditions over the past four decades have certainly squeezed more American family's home economies in such a way that most households now rely on two incomes.

### References

A2Z Homeschooling. (n.d.). *HSLDA and gun free school zone act*. Retrieved February 18, 2020, from https://a2zhomeschooling.com/main_articles/hslda_gun_free_school_zone_act/

Baidi, I. (2019). The role of parents' interests and attitudes in motivating them to home-school their children. *Journal of Social Studies Education Research, 10*(1), 156–177.

Beecher, C. (1835). *An essay on the education of female teachers.* Van Nostrand & Dwight.

Berliner, D. C., & Biddle, B. J. (1995). *The manufactured crisis: Myths, fraud, and the attack on America's public schools.* Addison-Wesley.

Berliner, D. C., & Glass, G. V. (2014). *50 myths and lies that threaten America's public schools: The real crisis in education.* Teachers College Press.

Brewer, T. J., & Cody, A. (2014). Teach for America: The neoliberal alternative to teacher professionalism. In J. A. Gorlewski, B. Porfilio, D. A. Gorlewski, & J. Hopkins (Eds.), *Effective or wise? Teaching and the meaning of professional dispositions in education* (pp. 77–94). Peter Lang.

Brewer, T. J., & Lubienski, C. (2017). Homeschooling in the United States: Examining the rationales for individualizing education. *Pro-Posições, 28*(2), 21–38.

Brewer, T. J., & Potterton, A. U. (2020). How market forces and erosion of education as a public good drive equity gaps wider. In M. Soskil (Ed.), *Flip the system us: How teachers can transform education and strengthen American democracy* (pp. 82–96). Routledge.

Brewer, T. J., & Swain, A. (2020). Operationalizing toxic ideology: How radical right-wing campus organizations undermine democratic engagement In K. deMarrais (Ed.), *Conservative philanthropies & organizations shaping U.S. educational policy & practice* (pp. 201–222). Myers Education Press.

Bryant, J. (2020). *Homeschooling movement sees opportunity during health calamity.* Retrieved April 7, 2020, from https://www.laprogressive.com/homeschooling-movement/

Bushak, L. (2014). *The 'STD hotspots' of America: Which states are most affected by chlamydia, gonorrhea, and aids?* Retrieved February 13, 2020, from https://www.medicaldaily.com/std-hotspots-america-which-states-are-most-affected-chlamydia-gonorrhea-and-aids-270761

Carter, J. H., & Lochte, H. A. (Eds.). (2017). *Teacher performance assessment and accountability reforms: The impacts of edtpa on teaching and schools.* Palgrave Macmillian.

CDC. (2017). *Over half of U.S. Teens have had sexual intercourse by age 18, new report shows.* Retrieved February 14, 2020, from https://www.cdc.gov/nchs/pressroom/nchs_press_releases/2017/201706_NSFG.htm

CDC. (n.d.). *Reproductive health: Teen pregnancy.* Retrieved February 13, 2020, from https://www.cdc.gov/teenpregnancy/about/index.htm

Children, H. s. I. (n.d.). *Home.* Retrieved February 17, 2020, from https://hsinvisiblechildren.org

Children's Hospital of Philadephia Researach Institute. (n.d.). *Gun violence: Facts and statistics.* Retrieved February 18, 2020, from https://injury.research.chop.edu/violence-prevention-initiative/types-violence-involving-youth/gun-violence/gun-violence-facts-and#.XkwQny3MzOQ

Coontz, S. (1992). *The way we never were: American families and the nostalgia trap*. Basic Books.

Council for the Accreditation of Educator Preparation. (n.d.). *History*. Retrieved March 23, 2015, from http://caepnet.org/about/history/

CRHE. (n.d.-a). *Homeschool notification*. Retrieved March 27, 2020, from https://responsiblehomeschooling.org/policy-issues/current-policy/notification/

CRHE. (n.d.-b). *Search: Abuse*. Retrieved February 17, 2020, from https://responsiblehomeschooling.org/?s=abuse&submit=Go

Cui, J., & Hanson, R. (2019). *Homeschooling in the United States: Results from the 2012 and 2016 parent and family involvement survey (PFI-NHES: 2012 and 2016)*. National Center for Education Statistics. Retrieved from https://nces.ed.gov/pubs2020/2020001.pdf

Dahlberg, L. L., Ikeda, R. M., & Kresnow, M. J. (2004). Guns in the home and risk of a violent death in the home: Findings from a national study. *American Journal of Epidemiology, 160*(10), 929–936.

deMarrais, K., Brewer, T. J., Atkinson, J. C., Herron, B., & Lewis, J. (2019). *Philanthropy, hidden strategy, and collective resistance: A primer for concerned educators*. Myers Education Press.

Fraser, J. (2014). *The school in the United States: A documented history*. Routledge.

Goldstein, D. (2014). *The teacher wars: A history of America's most embattled profession*. Doubleday.

Grady-Pawl, S. (2017). *Linking religion and teen pregnancy: There's a map for that*. Retrieved Februaray 13, 2020, from https://thehumanist.com/commentary/linking-religion-teen-pregnancy-theres-map

Henn, J. (2019). *Take the mystery out of homeschooling*. Paper presented at the Southeast Homeschool Expo, Atlanta, GA.

HHS. (n.d.). *Trends in teen pregnancy and childbearing*. Retrieved February 13, 2020, from https://www.hhs.gov/ash/oah/adolescent-development/reproductive-health-and-teen-pregnancy/teen-pregnancy-and-childbearing/trends/index.html

Howsam, R. B., Corrigan, D. C., Denemark, G. W., & Nash, R. J. (1976). *Educating a profession: Report of the bicentennial commission on education for the profession of teaching of the American association of college for teacher education*. U.S. Department of Health, Education & Welfare.

HSLDA. (n.d.). *Homeschool laws in your state*. Retrieved July 9, 2019, from https://hslda.org/content/laws/

Huseman, J. (2015). *Homeschooling regulations by state*. Retrieved July 9, 2019, from https://projects.propublica.org/graphics/homeschool

Jenna, B. (2009). *Teen birth rates highest in most religious states*. Retrieved February 13, 2020, from http://www.nbcnews.com/id/32884806/ns/health-childrens_health/t/teen-birth-rates-highest-most-religious-states/#.XkVaDy3MzOQ

Klein, N. (2007). *The shock doctrine: The rise of disaster capitalism*. Picador.

Kumashiro, K. (2012). *Bad teacher! How blaming teachers distorts the bigger picture.* Teachers College Press.

Kumashiro, K. (2015). *Review of proposed 2015 federal teacher preparation regulations.* National Education Policy Center. http://nepc.colorado.edu/thinktank/review-proposed-teacher-preparation

Kunzman, R. (2012). Education, schooling, and children's rights: The complexity of homeschooling. *Educational Theory, 62*(1), 75–89.

Levin, J., Mulhern, J., & Schunck, J. (2005). *Unintended consequences: The case for reforming the staffing rules in urban teachers union contracts.* The New Teacher Project.

Linsenbach, S. (2010). *The everything guide to homeschooling: All you need too create the best curriculum and learning environment for your child.* Adams Media.

Livingston, G., & Thomas, D. (2019). *Why is the teen birth rate falling?* Retrieved February 13, 2020, from https://www.pewresearch.org/fact-tank/2019/08/02/why-is-the-teen-birth-rate-falling/

Lubienski, C., & Lubienski, S. (2014). *The public school advantage: Why public schools outperform private schools.* The University of Chicago Press.

MacLean, N. (2017). *Democracy in chains: The deep history of the radical right's stealth plan for America.* Penguin Books.

Mathis, W. (2013). *Research-based options for education policymaking.* National Education Policy Center. http://nepc.colorado.edu/publication/options

Metzl, J. M. (2019). *Dying of whiteness: How the politics of racial resentment is killing America's heartland.* Basic Books.

Nichols, T. (2017). *The death of expertise: The campaign against established knowledge and why it matters.* Oxford University Press.

Pollack, K. C. (2018). *Report indicates a third of children removed from school to be homeschooled were involved in prior DCF abuse/neglect cases.* Retrieved February 17, 2020, from https://responsiblehomeschooling.org/report-indicates-a-third-of-children-removed-from-school-to-be-homeschooled-were-involved-in-prior-dcf-abuse-neglect-cases/

Prabhu, M. T. (2020). *Child abuse reporting in georgia down by half since schools closed amid virus.* Retrieved April 16, 2020, from https://www.ajc.com/news/state--regional-govt--politics/child-abuse-reporting-georgia-down-half-since-schools-closed-amid-virus/RKg3HzBy86Ai3QNq3jrZML/

Princiotta, D., Bielick, S., & Chapman, C. (2006). *Homeschooling in the United States: 2003: Statistical analysis report.* National Center for Education Statistics. https://nces.ed.gov/pubs2006/2006042.pdf

Rand, A. (1957/1999). *Atlas shrugged.* Penguin Random House.

Ravitch, D. (2010). *The death and life of the great American school system: How testing and choice are undermining education.* Basic Books.

Ravitch, D. (2013). *Reign of error: The hoax of the privatization movement and the danger to America's public schools.* Knopf.

Ray, B. D. (2019). *Research facts on homeschooling.* Retrieved August 5, 2019, from https://www.nheri.org/research-facts-on-homeschooling/

Redford, J., Battle, D., Bielick, S., & Grady, S. (2017). *Homeschooling in the United States: 2012.* National Center for Education Statistics. https://nces.ed.gov/pubs2016/2016096rev.pdf

Roth, D., & Swail, W. S. (2000). *Certification and teacher preparation in the United States.* Educational Policy Institute.

Rozyla, L. (2015). *Changes proposed to Florida's homeschool policies following girl's death.* Retrieved November 12, 2015, from http://www.abcactionnews.com/news/local-news/changes-proposed-to-floridas-homeschool-policies-following-girls-death

Schillinger, D., Ray, B. D., Knapp, K., & Newman, J. (n.d.). *Homeschool vs. public school: The ultimate showdown.* Retrieved February 17, 2020, from https://homeeducator.com/homeschool-vs-public-school/

Stevens, M. L. (2001). *Kingdom of children: Culture and controversy in the homeschooling movement.* Princeton University Press.

Stewart, K. (2019). *The power worshippers: Inside the dangerous rise of religious nationalism.* Bloomsbury Publishing.

Students Matter. (2014). *Vergara v. California case summary.* Retrieved September 8, 2015, from http://studentsmatter.org/our-case/vergara-v-california-case-summary/

The New Teacher Project. (2015). *The mirage: Confronting the hard truth about our quest for teacher development.* The New Teacher Project.

Tuccille, J. D. (2019). *Homeschooling produces better-educated, more-tolerant kids. Politicians hate that.* Retrieved February 17, 2020, from https://reason.com/2019/01/22/homeschooling-produces-better-students/

Urban, W. J., & Wagoner, J. L. (2009). *American education: A history* (4th ed.). Routledge.

Vergara v. California (Superior Court of the State of California 2014).

Westover, T. (2018). *Educated: A memoir.* Random House.

Whitaker, W., & Burns, J. (2019). Toward the end of teacher education? edTPA as the new guardian sentinel of teacher certification. In T. J. Brewer & C. A. Lubienski (Eds.), *Becoming a teacher in an age of reform: Global lessons for teacher preparation and the teaching profession* (pp. 67–90). Teacher's College Press.

CHAPTER 3

# Religious Rationales for Homeschooling

Though, the appointment of Secretary of Education Betsy DeVos brought with it an overt agenda to not only dismantle public education as much as possible in favor of private schools, charter schools, and homeschooling but, to the extent that public schools could not be eradicated, DeVos and similar thinkers are determined to bring their particular religiosity into public schools. Case in point, DeVos stated that she wanted to use public schools to "build God's kingdom" (Rizga, 2017; Wermund, 2016). While DeVos represents some of these efforts at the federal level, state-level politicians have sought to bring religion and White supremacy into public schools. Cynthia Dunbar, a homeschooling parent and former member of the Texas School Board, is a good example of these efforts at the state level. Dunbar was among the leading champions for pushing to reshape Texas curriculum and textbooks (which are largely catered to Texas curriculum) into a narrow White Christian disposition hoping that changes in the science and social studies curriculum would more closely align with her belief that the United States was specifically designed to follow the Bible along a White-Protestant theocracy as explicated in her self-published book: "One Nation Under God: How the Left is Trying to Erase What Made us Great" (Dunbar, 2008). To the end that she believes the "left" is undermining the United States, during her time as a member of the Board, Dunbar penned an Op-Ed arguing that then President Barack Obama was secretly working with Islamic terrorists to help them plan and execute a terrorist attack in the United States in an effort to dismantle America (Associated Press, 2008).

Of course, Dunbar is not the only example of how these types of efforts continue to be promoted in state legislators as conservatives push for laws allowing for the overt teaching and support of Bible-based classes (Ryan, 2019; Sheasley & Jonsson, 2019), official prayer in school, and even efforts to shield students from losing points on assignments if their answers are justified by their religious beliefs rather than science (Hancock, 2019). For example, a fundamentalist Christian student in a seventh grade biology class taking a test that asked students about the age of the earth or the origin of species could answer that the earth is 6,000 years old and that evolution is "fake news" based on his or her religion would not lose points. I intentionally use the phrase "fake news" here given the rise of the phrase as a result of Donald Trump and, in the case of his most ardent supporters, the penchant for Evangelical Christians to assert that scientific facts somehow represent a concerted conspiracy from the

© KONINKLIJKE BRILL NV, LEIDEN, 2021 | DOI: 10.1163/9789004457096_003

scientific community to downplay, diminish, or challenge their belief in the existence of God – a characteristic of the church dating back to the Inquisition and the Scientific Revolution.

Christian Reconstructionism, the philosophy and ideology behind much of the religious right's support of homeschooling is "a theocratic movement seeking to infuse our society at all levels with a biblical worldview" (Stewart, 2019, p. 103). In order to realize the goal of reshaping society to reflect specific, often narrow, Protestant-Evangelical-Conservative worldview, many use homeschooling as a method of insulating the next generation of change agents away from the influence of secular public schools. Katherine Stewart traces the growth of Christian Reconstructionism and its political connections to the Reagan administration to the Religious Roundtable's National Affairs Briefing in 1980 that propelled Regan to the status he held, and still holds, among the religious right. Reagan's rise to the presidency brought with him the influence of the religious right, including one of the most notable advocates for Christian Reconstructionism, R. J. Rushdoony. In fact,

> The Christian homeschooling movement, which has played a role in indoctrinating fresh generations in a 'biblical' worldview is explicitly indebted to Rushdoony's work. The Quiverfull movement, which encourages ultraconservative Christian couples to produce as many children as possible, was in large part inspired by Rushdoony. (Stewart, 2019, pp. 103–104)

While one rationale for homeschooling is, and has always been, decidedly a religious response to what some families see as a public school system far too secular for their children, the very practice of homeschooling itself has continually been leveraged as a mechanism to affect cultural and policy changes in the broader society. In fact, the push to "supplant public schools with home schooling or religious instruction" (Phillips, 2006, p. 371) is in alignment with the theocratic tendencies of the Christian Reconstruction movement. Kieryn Darkwater opined on the close connection that Evangelical Christianity and far-right political ideology has had on both homeschooling and politics itself – noting that homeschooling can, and has, been leveraged to promote far-right wing political ideologies. Further, Darkwater acknowledges that she was raised in a homeschooling family that adhered to the Evangelical movement known as "Quiverfull" that "measures a mother's spiritual resolve by the number of children she raises, each one an arrow in the quiver of God's army" (Joyce, 2006) which also carries with it tenants of racial understandings that seek to maintain the United States as a White majority populace as Joyce notes,

> Population is a preoccupation for many Quiverfull believers, who trade
> statistics on the falling white birthrate in European countries like Germany
> and France. Every ethnic conflict becomes evidence for their worldview:
> Muslim riots in France, Latino immigration in California, Sharia law in
> Canada. The motivations aren't always racist, but the subtext of "race sui-
> cide" is often there. (Joyce, 2006, para. 13)

In many ways, the preoccupation with an ideology like Quiverfull is in alignment with other right-wing White supremacist dispositions and ideologies
that promote beliefs such as "White replacement theory" or "White genocide"
known among alt-right circles as "The Great Replacement" (Charlton, 2019;
Schwartzburg, 2019a, 2019b). And while it may be easy, or desirable to dis-
miss these racist dispositions as peripheral, they have, in many ways, become
mainstreamed and condoned through high-profile individuals such as Trump's
senior policy advisor Stephen Miller who was long believed to be a White
supremacist – a fact confirmed through the release of racist emails he sent
to the far-right news/blog Breitbart organization (Southern Poverty Law Center, 2019; Wilson, 2019) and of notable interest as Miller oversees the Trump
administration's anti-immigrant efforts (note, however, that Trump has stated
he would prefer more immigrants from Norway – a majority White nation). In
her exploration of the religious nationalism practices by many on the political
right and evangelical circles, Katherine Stewart points out the importance of
interpreting the bible as specifically "pro-natalist" as adherents believe that

> government policy should 'incentivize population growth' [Ralph
> Drollinger] argues, quoting Psalm 127:5, 'Blessed is the man whose quiver
> is full of them.' The same passage is a favorite among conservative Chris-
> tians who eschew birth control in their pursuit of very large families.
> (Stewart, 2019, p. 50)

Drollinger, as Stewart documents, leads a weekly Bible study at the White
House in which DeVos, Vice President Mike Pence, and Secretary of State Mike
Pompeo, among others, are in regular attendance. This commitment to having
as many children as possible and homeschooling them stands in stark opposition to perceptions of public schools that are held by many fundamentalist
evangelical Christians and a desire to not only reinforce narrow religious ideology within the family but to extend that beyond and into society through
politics that resembles theocracy. Specifically,

> Rushdoony advocated a return to "biblical" law in America. The Bible,
> says Rushdoony, commands Christians to exercise absolute dominion

over the earth and all of its inhabitants. Women are destined by God to be subordinate to men; men are destined to be ruled by a spiritual aristocracy of right-thinking, orthodox Christian clerics; and the federal government is an agent of evil. Public education, in Rushdoony's reading of the Bible, is a threat to civilization, for it "basically trains women to be men," and represents "primitivism," "chaos," and "a vast 'integration into the void.'" (Stewart, 2019, p. 104)

Within this mindset, public schools are to be avoided by way of homeschooling, wives/mothers should remain at home in their "wifely" roles – which facilitates the opportunity to homeschool, families that homeschool for these religious rationales should have as many children as possible so that they can then become a growing army intent on taking "back" control of government and enforcing religious-based laws and practices. And this has been going on for a while as "Evangelical conservatives started taking over their local republican parties and founding organizations like Operation Rescue, Homeschool Legal Defense Association, Family Research Council[,] and Focus on the Family, just to name a few" (Darkwater, 2017, para. 5). Darkwater goes on to argue that the HSLDA and its sister organization, Generation Joshua, was founded to

> train [homeschooled children] to fight in what the Christofascists have been calling the 'Culture Wars.' It's a loose and ambiguous term that basically means anything or anyone that doesn't align with this very specific view of Christianity must not be allowed to continue. (Darkwater, 2017, para. 7)

Additionally, Darkwater suggests that to accomplish this goal,

> you overturn *Roe v. Wade, Griswold v. Connecticut, Brown v. Board of Education* and *Bob Jones v. The United States*. Each of these decisions currently protects reproductive rights or non-discrimination based on race. As retribution, you amend the Constitution to discriminate against queers, trans people, women and people of color. Then, you make laws legislating morality. The only way to do this is to infiltrate the government; so Generation Joshua, TeenPact and other organizations exist to indoctrinate and recruit homeschooled youth who have ample free time to participate in politics. (Darkwater, 2017, para. 8)

And while some from within this religious doctrine are focused on doing what they can to shape public schools into the religious landscape they imagine such

54 CHAPTER 3

as DeVos's goal of using public schools to "build God's kingdom," the agenda is not limited to revamping public education. The goal is to,

> Take Back The Country For Christ. This was the mantra we heard. This was our mission. This is how we were to win: Outbreed, Outvote, Outactivate. Every class, every event, every pastor or guest speaker reiterated this, choosing to risk the 501c3 status of their church to push their agenda. To take back the country for Christ, we needed to outbreed, outvote and outactivate the other side, thus saith The Lord. (Darkwater, 2017, para. 12)

Some of this requires a reinterpretation or rewriting of U.S. history as,

> Self-proclaimed constitutional lawyer Michael Farris, the founder of HSLDA, and revisionist historian **David Barton** have spent years twisting their interpretation of the U.S. Constitution as some kind of God-breathed document into the minds of parents and their families who will just believe what they say because they're "Good Christians." They don't necessarily practice critical thought, are dissuaded from looking at the Constitution themselves without a law degree and don't bother to read history from all angles, relying only on the whitewashed Christian versions of the Constitution and our founding. (Darkwater, 2017, para. 16)

And, seemingly, the close connection between Republican ideology and homeschooling is useful as "Republicans have a vast network of homeschoolers that HSLDA and others have given them to tap into as a source of free labor. Republicans in state governments are lax on homeschooling oversight because their Get Out The Vote base is made of homeschoolers thanks to Generation Joshua and Teenpact" further quoting Republican Senator Tom Cotton who praised the efforts of homeschooled students in their efforts to get people to vote. It is worth noting that the HSLDA maintains a page dedicated to bringing its member's attention to laws that should be supported or opposed along with a breakdown of state and federal campaigns of note (HSLDA, n.d.).

The waging of the Culture Wars at the direction of homeschooling families and the push to view the Constitution through whitewashed Christian ideology was seen as the Texas School Board revamped its science and social studies curriculum standards in 2012. The school board was largely comprised of fundamental Evangelical Christians, led by Don McLeroy, and sought to reimagine the standards to align with a narrow view of Christianity and to promote a Biblical worldview (Thurman et al., 2012). Board member Cynthia Dunbar, who later went on to become the chairperson of the Board, helped push through some of the more notable right-wing evangelical rewrites of the social studies and science curriculum. Of interest here is that Dunbar homeschooled all three of her children. Returning to the notion of Quiverfull, Joyce notes that adherents are interested in the,

> worldly effects that a Christian embrace of Quiverfull could bring. "When at the height of the Reagan Revolution," they write, "the conservative faction in Washington was enforced [*sic*] with squads of new conservative congressmen, legislators often found themselves handcuffed by lack of like-minded staff. There simply weren't enough conservatives trained to serve in Washington in the lower and middle capacities." But if just 8 million American Christian couples began supplying more "arrows for the war" by having six children or more, they propose, the Christian-right ranks could rise to 550 million within a century ("assuming Christ does not return before then"). They like to ponder the spiritual victory that such numbers could bring: both houses of Congress and the majority of state governor's mansions filled by Christians; universities that embrace creationism; sinful cities reclaimed for the faithful; and the swift blows dealt to companies that offend Christian sensibilities. (Joyce, 2006, para. 32)

The belief in White homeschooling families to have as many children as possible is a notable characteristic of many American homeschooling families. Indeed, during the opening session of the Homeschooling Expo in Atlanta, the first keynote speaker (a White woman) noted that she had 7 children (Henn, 2019) – to which, the entire audience cheered and applauded loudly. Moreover, the practice of Quiverfull and homeschooling became mainstream with the popular rise of the show "19 Kids and Counting" which brought viewers into the home of the Duggar family comprised of husband, wife, and 19 children.

Aside from religious lifestyle practices related to Quiverfull and the connected political agendas that arise from within, many families that homeschool do so in an effort to situate subject curriculum to align with myopic religious doctrines. This can often take the form of a parent's desire to prevent children from being exposed to lessons on evolution, dinosaurs, and sex education to name a few. Anecdotally, I have understood the topic of avoiding evolution to be among the top curriculum rationales to homeschool in the name of religion. That is, parents who interpret their religious texts as being incompatible with the theory of evolution, or rather, evolution to be incompatible with their beliefs on the origins of Earth and humans, seek to prevent their children from exposure to the scientific theories that, on the face of it, might present the opportunity for their children to question creationism and, by extension, Christianity itself.

56                                                                    CHAPTER 3

Megan Fox, a fundamentalist Evangelical Christian and outspoken Trump supporter who homeschools her children, produces a myriad of videos on her YouTube channel that has approximately 4,000 subscribers. Her most popular video, viewed nearly 1.3 million times at the time of this writing, is an "audit" of the Field Museum's exhibit on evolution (Fox, 2014). In her video, Fox explores the Field's exhibitions showcasing her commitment to anti-intellectualism claiming that the "facts" that are presented are made up. Below is a transcript of the opening minutes of Fox's "audit" of the "Evolving Earth" exhibit beginning with signage on evolution:

Fox:                        I don't know how to say this word so I'm just going to pretend that I know how to say it

Camera Operator:            eukaryotes

Fox:                        eukaryotes? Here's another interesting thing. Now they're going to tell you that this is how the evolution of a cell began.

Fox:                        [reading from the signage] Eukaryotes are different from other cells [skipping the reading of "prokaryotes"] because they have a nucleus, which contains the cell's DNA, blah-blah-blah [while hand gesturing for talking].

Fox:                        [skipping a few lines] At first, all eukaryotes were single-celled, and many still are today. What? If many still are *today*, then that would support the theory that they have never changed, that they have always been as they are today. Not that they started someplace else and then are here, they were always this, and still are today. This makes no sense ... none of this makes any sense.

Fox:                        [at another wall display] How do they know this? They're talking about 470 million years ago, these are just guesses off of the top of their heads.

Fox:                        [pointing to the word First] First – I love how they write these things ... this is what happened for sure, for sure, this is what happened first. Listen to how dumb this sounds! [Fox then reads from the display] "First, the ozone layer – formed when oxygen began to accumulate in Earth's atmosphere – provided protection from the sun's harmful radiation. Only water had provided this protection before." *How do you know this*? This is just a fairy tale. They're just making it up but we want the whole scientific community and everyone else to believe this.

Yet, Fox is not alone in this type of thinking that can be endemic among many who homeschool due to myopic religious and anti-intellectual beliefs. One of the most striking and disturbing that was offered during the Homeschool Expo in Atlanta was a session entitled: "The Ten Things All Future Mathematicians and Scientists Must Know (But are Rarely Taught)." From the title, it is not a far stretch to interpret the session as promoting anti-intellectualism by suggesting that those with scientific and mathematic expertise are, somehow, lacking the requisite insights and knowledge needed for their jobs as it is "rarely taught." The session description read as follows:

> Mathematicians and scientists have been closely tied to many famous disasters. The Challenger explosion, the failure of the Mars Explorer, and the Kansas City Hyatt Regency walkway collapse all involved thinking errors. Our future mathematicians and scientists must know how to prevent tragedies such as these from occurring. Because science and mathematics instruction is often *dominated by facts and calculation*, children are rarely exposed to these important concepts. You will leave this session with many high interest stories and activities that will fascinate your children and show them the strong connections between math and science and the world we live in. (Zaccaro, 2019, emphasis added)

Clearly, there is a quite a bit to unpack here. First, there is, again, an overt foundation of anti-intellectualism and skepticism of expertise. There is a subtle hinting that experts allow their knowledge to blind them of more accurate or purer insights that, were that not the case, would not result in disasters. Secondly, the session speaker engages in some very specific cherry-picking of what were decidedly terrible disasters as one-off outliers to suggest that they are representative of a larger systemic problem within the STEM landscape. Not mentioned, of course, are the hundreds of other successful lunches and landings of the space shuttles, successful Apollo missions (many of which resulted in learning from early disasters), the successful landing and operations of other Mars rovers, and thousands upon thousands of bridges and walkways that have not collapsed. Wrought within this anti-intellectual framework and animosity towards those perceived to be intellectual elites is a mistrust and disbelief in facts and calculations. Obviously this is made abundantly clear from the session description above but such a disposition runs rampant within political and religious circles that interpret facts and calculations that do not align with preconceived political or religious beliefs as "fake news" while promoting ideas such as "truth isn't truth," and "alternative facts" (Kwong, 2018). The mantra that scientists and experts cannot be trusted was a foundational component of many of the conference sessions. The summary for a session entitled, "Jurassic Reality: Dinosaurs and the Most Asked Questions!" read as follows:

> People of all ages are captivated by dinosaurs. Unfortunately, evolutionists use dinosaurs to indoctrinate the young and the old with an earth history that includes millions of years but has no room for the Bible. This presentation will show the power of a person's starting assumptions (or "worldview") when interpreting past events, and will define the different types of sciences used in investigating the world around us, with a thorough exploration of these enigmatic lizards. Let's take dinosaurs to the Bible and see what God's word has to say about them! (Sarfati, 2019)

A notable right-wing, anti-science Christian persona in this landscape is Ken Ham who famously debated Bill Nye on the topic of evolution and is the director of the Ark Encounter (a built-to-biblical-scale replica of Noah's ark). In addition to his work related to the Ark Encounter, Ham produces or appears across a myriad of Christian-based educational curriculum for homeschooling families. One such program from Ham's "Answers in Genesis" organization is a DVD titled "Dinosaurs, Genesis & the Gospel" where Ham lectures on dinosaurs while Buddy Davis sings original bible-based songs on the same topics (Ham & Davis, 2004). Below is a transcript of the sample portion of Ham's lecturer which was recorded in front of an auditorium of parents and their children:

> *Well, boys and girls, put your hand up if you've heard the word evolution. Oh boy, just about everyone put their hand up. Put your hands down. Put your hand up if you've heard that dinosaurs lived millions of years ago. Dear, oh dear, hands down. Put your hand up if you've heard that people came from ape-like creatures or something like that. You know, I think just about everyone in the world has heard those things. I want to tell you right from the start here this morning that neither Buddy nor myself, we don't believe in evolution. Evolution is the idea that some people have to explain life and our God. You know, when you came in here this morning did you look at this building and say, 'wow, it got here by an explosion in a brick factory? You don't think that? No, you know somebody designed this building and I certainly don't believe*

RELIGIOUS RATIONALES FOR HOMESCHOOLING 59

*that life came about by chance random processes millions of years ago in some soup in the sea, life was formed and then one kind of animal changes into another ape-like creatures and then into people until finally here we are in Pennsylvania. I don't believe that all, do you? ... I don't believe that dinosaurs lived millions of years ago. And I certainly don't believe, and neither does Buddy, that you came from ape-like creatures. I mean, in fact, did your grandfather look like that?* [shows a caricature composite photo mixing a human face with an ape's face – to which the children laugh], *I don't think so. Does your grandmother look like that?* [shows the same picture now with makeup – to which the children laugh louder]. (Ham & Davis, 2004)

Ham goes on to reinforce that he believes that the Bible is the "history book of the universe" – a point he makes the children parrot. The picture of the workbook created by Ham and Davis that accompanies the video is a smiling tyrannosaurus rex smiling while holding a glowing Bible.

While many homeschooling families purchase curriculum designed specifically for homeschooling – often with the additional feature of centering religious instruction or religion-based alternative perspectives on settled science – there are a plethora of online and free curriculum resources available. Still, many of these resources center religion. For example, the "Easy Peasy All-In-One Homeschool" site provides content and lesson planning for homeschooling families from pre-K through high school (Easy Peasy All-In-One Homeschool, n.d.-b). Notably, the first lessons for pre-K students center on using content from the McGuffey's Readers which were widely used in common schools between the mid 1800s to the mid 1900s to reinforce a religious and Bible-based orientation to reading. The site's owner is clear that the purpose of homeschooling and the curriculum provided is to not only advance a Christian perspective but also to provide insights into how to argue against mainstream scientific insights that are interpreted as not in alignment with a particular and specific interpretation of the Bible that is not shared among all Christians. The site notes that,

This is a Christian curriculum. Most things are not overtly Christian, but I do point to the Bible from time to time in literature, science, history, etc. and seek to promote a biblical worldview. I also believe in a literal six-day creation. I do choose to use materials that talk about millions of years because it is what's available, and it's useful for our children to know what's taught out there so they can be intelligent in a response to it. I do address it to varying degrees when it comes up. (Easy Peasy All-In-One Homeschool, n.d.-a)

60                                                                                    CHAPTER 3

However, while some attention is given to scientific theory surrounding the age of the earth – if only to learn how to "respond" to it, the curriculum designer specifically avoids exposing students to religions other than Christianity. For example,

> I also don't study false religion [in the homeschooling curriculum]. My children know the basics about it, but you won't find me teaching them about the gods of Ancient Egypt for example. They will know they had a false religion and worshiped other gods, but we don't need to learn all of their names and what they looked like. It also makes me careful around things like Native Americans and their spirit guides, etc. Not all literature the children will read is pure in every way. But, that's a way to talk about the world and choices and consequences and how we should react in certain circumstances ...

Ensuring that children are not exposed to competing understandings of the world – religious or otherwise – should raise significant questions about the quality of education and its ability to prepare children to become adults in a multicultural world. Occasionally, a local or national news story brings attention to Christian parents who are irate at the suggestion that their student in public school be exposed to any religion other than Protestant Christianity. This takes on the form of overt discussions and learning related to world religions but also surrounding innocuous practices such as yoga because it is understood as being explicitly anti-Christian and schools that offer yoga amounts "to a tacit endorsement of a non-Christian belief system" (Rojas, 2020). Tucker Carlson, the host of a wildly popular primetime show on Fox News, held a segment with two mothers who were protesting a New Jersey public school for their teaching of the five pillars of Islam. According to them, this amounted to a liberal attempt to brainwash students into becoming Muslim – a disposition that generally aligned with rhetoric on Fox News during the Obama administration given the network's promotion of the conspiracy theories that Obama was a secret Muslim attempting to bring Sharia Law into the United States by indoctrinating students. Conspiracy theories aside, the parents from New Jersey insisted, quite vehemently, that the public school was pushing Islam onto students and had never covered Christianity. Despite such claims, the state standard for the social studies curriculum in the 6th grade which is nearly identical to all social studies standards for middle and high school social studies and history. The standard reads,

> Compare and contrast the tenets of various world religions that developed in or around this time period (i.e., Buddhism, Christianity, Confu-

cianism, Hinduism, Islam, Judaism, Sikhism, and Taoism), their patterns of expansion, and their responses to the current challenges of globalization. (New Jersey Department of Education, 2014, p. 37)

Contrary to the self-selected and self-isolated curriculum that refuses to explore the tenets of world religions (even those that are connected to Christianity as Abrahamic faiths – e.g., Islam and Judaism), is the public school curriculum that promotes a broad range of skills necessary for citizenship. In fact, according to the New Jersey Department of Education, the mission of its social studies curriculum is to provide "learners with the knowledge, skills, and perspectives needed to become active, informed citizens and contributing members of local, state, national, and global communities in the digital age" (Plein, n.d.). Moreover, the curriculum seeks to foster a population that,

- Is civic minded, globally aware, and socially responsible.
- Exemplifies fundamental values of American citizenship through active participation in local and global communities.
- Makes informed decisions about local, state, national, and global events based on inquiry and analysis.
- Considers multiple perspectives, values diversity, and promotes cultural understanding.
- Recognizes the implications of an interconnected global economy.
- Appreciates the global dynamics between people, places, and resources.
- Utilizes emerging technologies to communicate and collaborate on career and personal matters with citizens of other world regions. (Plein, n.d.)

Compare this disposition, again, to the possibility that homeschooling curriculum can, and often does, cherry-picking topics that suit a specific world-view or sterilized version of history. The Easy Peasy online homeschooling curriculum avoids some videos surrounding WWII "because I didn't want those images in front of their eyes, even if they are truth" (Easy Peasy All-In-One Homeschool, n.d.-a). But this selectivity is not limited to historical events as it exists even surrounding the Biblical orientation of the curriculum by cherry-picking the nicer portions of the Bible in an effort to avoid the more difficult sections or context of the text,

One final note about the Bible curriculum: I don't have them read *everything*. For example, when I put up Sodom and Gomorrah, they read that it was destroyed because of their great sin, but they don't read the part about what the people there died. And I stopped before Lot's daughters decide they need his help to continue the family line. You can't avoid it all; I mean, Jacob has twelve sons, but it's not hard to skip over what happened to their sister Dinah. (Easy Peasy All-In-One Homeschool, n.d.-a)

Another popular Christian curriculum available to homeschooling parents is produced by "My Father's World." In addition to the curriculum website, the organization mails periodic book catalogues much in the way that academic presses do announcing new textbooks. The approach offered by My Father's World "combines the best of Charlotte Mason's ideas, classical education, and unit studies with a biblical worldview and global focus. By keeping God's Word central, we partner with you to provide life-transforming, academic excellence with a Christian worldview" (My Father's World, n.d.-b). The provided high school "Ancient History and Literature" material is a "verse-by-verse reading of the entire Old Testament [that] encourages challenging, practical, daily application. Worldviews of ancient societies and their literature are studied and compared to a Biblical worldview" (My Father's World, n.d.-a).

In sum, the religious rationale to homeschool may be one of the most closely-held rationales given the power that religion plays in the lives of so many people (homeschooling or not). On the surface, public schools are seen as a direct threat to the ability to freely practice a chosen religion or a threat to the social morality that is intertwined within the religion. The goal for some using the religious rationale is to have their children avoid public schools while preparing them for a life of political and policy work that will reimagine public schools along myopic Protestant Evangelical lines as schools are seen as a mission field.

### References

Associated Press. (2008). *Education official stands by her Obama terror claim.* Retrieved November 19, 2019, from https://www.chron.com/news/houston-texas/article/Education-official-stands-by-her-Obama-terror-1772463.php#item-85307-tbla-2

Charlton, L. (2019). *What is the great replacement?* https://www.nytimes.com/2019/08/06/us/politics/grand-replacement-explainer.html

Darkwater, K. (2017). *I was trained for the culture wars in home school, awaiting someone like Mike Pence as a messiah.* Retrieved October 1, 2019, from https://www.autostraddle.com/i-was-trained-for-the-culture-wars-in-home-school-awaiting-someone-like-mike-pence-as-a-messiah-367057/?fbclid=IwAR3k1diy58NGbHyljo8ss4PVYnbSY5DAZotd484iGvbR9dofUdDcOyeXgrM

Dunbar, C. (2008). *One nation under god: How the left is trying to erase what made us great*. HigherLife Publishing.

Easy Peasy All-In-One Homeschool. (n.d.-a). *About/donate.* Retrieved February 25, 2020, from https://allinonehomeschool.com/about/

Easy Peasy All-In-One Homeschool. (n.d.-b). *Mcguffey primer.* Retrieved February 25, 2020, from https://allinonehomeschool.com/days-172-222-mcguffey-reader/

Fox, M. (2014). *Megan Fox audits the field museum's "evolving earth" exhibit.* Retrieved October 1, 2019, from https://www.youtube.com/watch?v=32mxZxv3dYM

Ham, K., & Davis, B. (2004). *Dinosaurs, genesis & the gospel, dvd.* Retrieved March 1, 2020, from https://www.christianbook.com/dinosaurs-genesis-the-gospel/ pd/00154X?event=Homeschool%7C1006429#customer_reviews

Hancock, L. (2019). *Ohio lawmakers clear bill critics say could expand religion in public schools.* Retrieved November 19, 2019, from https://www.cleveland.com/open/ 2019/11/ohio-lawmakers-clear-bill-allowing-students-to-turn-in-inaccurate-work-in-name-of-religion-second-anti-science-bill-in-a-week.html

Henn, J. (2019). *Take the mystery out of homeschooling.* Paper presented at the Southeast Homeschool Expo, Atlanga, GA.

HSLDA. (n.d.). *Current campaigns.* Retrieved March 26, 2020, from https://hslda.org/ content/legislation/?vvsrc=/Campaigns

Joyce, K. (2006). *'Arrows for the war'.* Retrieved October 1, 2019, from https://www.thenation.com/article/arrows-war/

Kwong, J. (2018). *'Truth isn't truth': Here are all the ways trump's administration has claimed facts are no longer real.* Retrieved July 29, 2019, from https://www.newsweek.com/truth-isnt-truth-here-are-all-ways-trumps-administration-has-claimed-facts-1081618

My Father's World. (n.d.-a). *9th–12th grade: Declare.* Retrieved February 27, 2020, from https://www.mfwbooks.com/cat/14/

My Father's World. (n.d.-b). *Curriculum for homeschool & christian schools.* Retrieved February 27, 2020, from https://www.mfwbooks.com/aapproach

New Jersey Department of Education. (2014). *New Jersey student learning standards for social studies.* Retrieved February 25, 2020, from https://www.nj.gov/education/ cccs/2014/ss/standards.pdf

Phillips, K. (2006). *American theocracy: The peril and politics of radical religion, oil, and borrowed money in the 21st century.* Penguin Books.

Plein, B. (n.d.). *New Jersey student learning standards: Social studies.* Retrieved February 25, 2020, from https://www.nj.gov/education/aps/cccs/ss/

Rizga, K. (2017). *Betsy DeVos wants to use America's schools to build "god's kingdom."* Retrieved February 12, 2018, from https://www.motherjones.com/politics/2017/01/ betsy-devos-christian-schools-vouchers-charter-education-secretary/

Rojas, R. (2020). *In a plan to bring yoga to Alabama schools, stretching is allowed. 'Namaste' isn't.* Retrieved March 10, 2020, from https://www.nytimes.com/2020/03/09/us/alabama-yoga-schools.html

Ryan, E. (2019). *There's a push for classes on the bible in public schools. And there's also a pushback.* Retrieved May 1, 2020, from https://www.cnn.com/2019/05/06/politics/bible-literacy-classes-legislation/index.html

Sarfati, J. (2019). *Jurassic reality: Dinosaurs and the most asked questions!* Paper presented at the Southeast Homeschool Expo, Atlanta, GA.

Schwartzburg, R. (2019a). *No, there isn't a White genocide.* Retrieved May 1, 2020, from https://www.jacobinmag.com/2019/09/white-genocide-great-replacement-theory

Schwartzburg, R. (2019b). *The 'White replacement theory' motivates alt-right killers the world over.* Retrieved May 1, 2020, from https://www.theguardian.com/commentisfree/2019/aug/05/great-replacement-theory-alt-right-killers-el-paso

Sheasley, C., & Jonsson, P. (2019). *More public schools are embracing the bible. Is it literature, or religion?* Retrieved May 1, 2020, from https://www.csmonitor.com/USA/Education/2019/0918/More-public-schools-are-embracing-the-Bible.-Is-it-literature-or-religion

Southern Poverty Law Center. (2019). *Stephen Miller: The Breitbart emails.* Retrieved November 19, 2019, from https://www.splcenter.org/stephen-miller-breitbart-emails

Stewart, K. (2019). *The power worshippers: Inside the dangerous rise of religious nationalism.* Bloomsbury Publishing.

Thurman, S. (Writer and Producer), Silver, P., & Wood, O. (Producers). (2012). *The revisionaries* [Film]. PBS.

Wermund, B. (2016). *Trump's education pick says reform can 'advance god's kingdom'.* Retrieved January 4, 2017, from http://www.politico.com/story/2016/12/betsy-devos-education-trump-religion-232150

Wilson, J. (2019). *Leaked emails reveal Trump aide Stephen Miller's White nationalist views.* Retrieved May 1, 2020, from https://www.theguardian.com/us-news/2019/nov/14/stephen-miller-leaked-emails-white-nationalism-trump

Zaccaro, E. (2019). *The ten things all future mathematicians and scientists must know (but are rarely taught).* Paper presented at the Southeast Homeschool Expo, Atlanta, GA.

CHAPTER 4

# Political Rationales for Homeschooling

The rationale to homeschool for political reasons can derive from many political philosophies and justifications – often, more than one. For many, public schools represent governmental overreach into our personal lives, student histories, medical and health records, financial records of the family, etc. Public schools, for some, represent an effort to control the masses through indoctrination into political ideals (e.g., Marxism, multiculturalism, diversity, etc.) and with scientific ideas that are interpreted as an affront to religious doctrines (e.g., evolution, climate change, sex education, etc.) but are perceived not singularly as religious issues but also political control. In the same vein, some see public schools as a challenge to notions of rugged individualism where it is – or ought to be – everyone for themselves (think stereotypical nostalgic views of Western-progressing pioneers). Circling back to the consideration of education understood as a public good that benefits the collective or as a private individualistic good, many understand homeschooling as a possibility to enact their political ideology that individuals (understood as individual families) are responsible for, and only unto, themselves. Within many circles, phrases such as "public education" and "public schools" are replaced with "government-controlled schools" to center the primary animosity towards public schools and favor of homeschooling as a political stance against what is seen as Statism and government overreach. Brian Ray (2016) suggests that,

> Whether the reader holds to a more statist or democratist [sic] worldview versus a classical liberal (cf. Rothbard, 1999) or biblical scriptural worldview will determine his or her thoughts about homeschooling in general and opinion about, in particular, whether the state should control private homeschooling. (p. 19)

A significant portion of this conversation is couched in the false dichotomy of "capitalism versus socialism, or freedom versus statism" (Rand, 1967, as cited inMacLean, 2017, p. 91). For others, such as the HSLDA, they oppose "any legislation that would increase regulation of homeschoolers" (HSLDA, n.d.) as any government oversight of homeschooling is understood, politically, as anathema to the rationale of homeschooling. This may also explain why we continue to know so little about who is homeschooling and for what purposes. The data that the National Center of Education Statistics – a government agency – notes

© KONINKLIJKE BRILL NV, LEIDEN, 2021 | DOI: 10.1163/9789004457096_004

that the "non-response rate [for its surveys] is higher for the homeschool survey than others" (Silva, 2018). While NCES is not a partisan agency, it is, by extension, part of the government and a lack of engagement can be part of the disposition towards eschewing government "intrusion" into private lives (see, for instance, Westover, 2018).

While Lubienski and Brewer argued that the public has a "responsibility to ensure a diverse socialization that is innate and necessary within a democracy" (Lubienski & Brewer, 2014, p. 144), homeschooling advocate Brian Ray of the NHERI pushed back suggesting that Lubienksi and Brewer,

> imply that homeschooling that is free of state control is a threat to their statist belief system. That is, Lubienski and Brewer want to use the state to control education to mold children's minds and worldviews to be socialized according to their personal vision of the good and right society. Further, neo-Marxist hopes show up in their concern that homeschooling will not right the wrongs – as they claim state-run schooling does – of certain "social inequities" that come with the particular family into which certain children are born (e.g., Lubienski & Brewer, p. 145). (Ray, 2016, p. 19)

In alignment with a commitment to libertarian rugged individualism, Ray claims that the aim of public schools to provide all students with a diverse socialization experience (which would include interactions with myriad of types of students and a broad curriculum), is tantamount to state-based control and Marxist indoctrination. And while I have been clear here that public schools have not fully realized its aim to provide equitable opportunities for all students, the point remains that public schools have the best possibility and opportunity for such goals. In Ray's summary of our claim above, he wrongly claims that such dispositions towards the opportunities as they exist between public schools and homeschooling amounts to Marxism. Our claim, in more detail, was,

> Finding roots in the neo-liberal ideologies of Milton Friedman, homeschool advocates and parents often view state-run schools as naturally ineffective and inefficient. Yet, state-run schools are likely more equipped to promote equality and diversity – a central concern of a pluralistic democracy – rather than the homogeneous environment of the family. Moreover, while there is some truth in views that government institutions can limit opportunities for some groups, state-run schools serve as a source of liberation for some groups, expanding opportunity for many

who would not otherwise have advantages from their home lives and providing and creating a sanctuary for those in more oppressive home environments. (Lubienski & Brewer, 2014, p. 145)

Put plainly, if the aim of our society is the maintenance of a pluralistic democracy, then by its very definition, homeschooling – which is nearly entirely homogeneous in nature – is less suited than public schools – which is more heterogeneous in nature – at facilitating the means by, and through, which such a society is maintained. But, the concept of a pluralistic democracy is specifically anathema to some of the politics notable among the homeschooling culture. Finding Biblical justification for slavery allowed Protestant evangelicals such as Rushdoony – a "powerful advocate for the Christian and home-school movements across America" (Stewart, 2019, p. 122) – to justify political stances that reinforced racial hierarchies in society and the schools that reinforced them by pushing back against pluralism. Specifically,

> Rushdoony amplified the message, arguing that the "government school" has "leveled its guns at God and family." "Liberal education is inevitably pluralistic," he lamented. "It would follow that Southerners are clearly wrong in resisting integration of white and Negro pupils." The implication here was that they were, in fact, right to have resisted integration. In Rushdoony's view, there was nothing wrong in principle with segregation. (Stewart, 2019, p. 118)

In considering the reasons that many homeschooling parents give to why they homeschool, Homeschooler and author of the book "Socialize Like a Homeschooler" and blogger at "Hifalutin Homeschooler" Jennifer Cabrera argues that many homeschooling families have, for too long, answered such questions from a position of political correctness often responding with, "It's what is best for our family." Couched in the conservative disposition of animus towards "PC language," Cabrera suggests that such answers are a "cop out" that should be avoided. What she suggests is that homeschooling parents be more honest and proud of their choice to homeschool that, in her case, was rationalized by wanting to be in control of their family's schedule, ensuring that their children were not exposed to bullying, school shootings, societal moral decline, and learning to think rather than "regurgitate facts for a test" while allowing the family to "follow God's instruction to educate our kids to live a Christian life" (Hifalutin Homeschooler, 2018). While Cabrera includes multiple "honest" reasons for why families may homeschool, much of the justifications are presented in response to what is understood as bad government. She claims that "homeschooling continues to grow as public education continues to spiral downward and our government becomes more contemptuous of the family unit ..." (Hifalutin Homeschooler, 2018). For Cabrera, the "non-politically correct" reasons that she and others homeschool are:

1. We like to be in control of our schedule and what values our kids learn.
2. To ensure our kids are loved and safe from bullies and school shootings.
3. We want our kids to get a top quality, personalized education.
4. So our kids will learn to think and reason, not just regurgitate facts for a test.
5. Our kids need time with their father, who they would otherwise never see.
6. It is best for our family.
7. The time with our kids will go by fast and we want to be together.
8. We want to follow God's instruction to educate our kids to live a Christian life.
9. Freedom!
10. We have seen the downward spiral of the education system, societies morals, and the family unit, and we don't want it influencing our children. (i.e. We've seen the village ...). (Hifalutin Homeschooler, 2018)

The term "values" in the first rationale is quite broad. While it can include religious values, those are listed separately later in the list. As a result, it is not beyond the scope of reason that values here mean political values. Other rationales above such as "Freedom!," understandings of policies that may influence changes in the education system that are seen as threatening morals, and testing all reflect political decisions. Of the "100 Reasons to Homeschool Your Kids," below are those that fall under the realm of political rationale:

*Political/Economic*
1. Homeschooling has wide bipartisan appeal.
2. Religious freedom may be important to many homeschooling families, but it is not the primary reason they choose to homeschool. "Concern about the school environment, such as safety, drugs, or negative peer pressure" is the top motivator according to federal data.
3. Fear of school shootings and widespread bullying are other concerns that are prompting more families to consider the homeschooling option.

4. Some parents choose homeschooling because they are frustrated by Common Core curriculum frameworks and frequent testing in public schools.

5. It will also prevent schools from surreptitiously collecting and tracking data on your child's mental health.

6. And you can actually enjoy lunch with them rather than being banned from the school cafeteria.

7. Your kids don't have to walk through metal detectors, past armed police officers, and into locked classrooms in order to learn.

8. You can avoid bathroom wars and let your kids go to the bathroom wherever and whenever they want—without raising their hand to ask for permission.

9. Schooling was for the Industrial Age, but unschooling is for the future.

10. With robots doing more of our work, we need to rely more on our distinctly human qualities, like curiosity and ingenuity, to thrive in the Innovation Era.

11. Today's teens aren't working in part-time or summer jobs like they used to. Homeschooling can offer time for valuable teen work experience.

12. It can also provide the opportunity to cultivate teen entrepreneurial skills.

13. By forming authentic connections with community members, homeschoolers can take advantage of teen apprenticeship programs.

14. Some apprenticeship programs have a great track record on helping homeschoolers build important career skills and get great jobs.

15. Homeschooling could be the "smartest way to teach kids in the 21st century," according to *Business Insider*.

16. But college doesn't need to be the only pathway to a meaningful adult life and livelihood. Many lucrative jobs don't require a college degree, and companies like Google and Apple have dropped their degree requirements.

17. In fact, more homeschooling families from the tech community in Silicon Valley and elsewhere are choosing to homeschool their kids.

18. Some of these hybrid homeschool programs are public charter schools that are free to attend and actually give families access to funds for homeschooling.

19. Other education choice mechanisms, like Education Savings Accounts (ESAs) and tax-credit scholarship programs, are expanding to include homeschoolers, offering financial assistance to those families who need and want it.

20. Some states allow homeschoolers to fully participate in their local school sports teams and extracurricular activities.
21. Your homeschooled kids will probably be able to name at least one right protected by the First Amendment of the US Constitution, something 37 percent of adults who participated in a recent University of Pennsylvania survey couldn't do.
22. Research suggests that homeschoolers are more politically tolerant than others.
23. In spite of ongoing efforts to regulate homeschoolers, US homeschooling is becoming less regulated.
24. That's because homeschooling parents are powerful defenders of education freedom.
25. Homeschooling is one way to get around regressive compulsory schooling laws and put parents back in charge of their child's education.
26. It can free children from coercive, test-driven schooling.
27. It is one education option among many to consider as more parents opt-out of mass schooling.
28. Homeschooling is the ultimate school choice.
29. It is inspiring education entrepreneurship to disrupt the schooling status quo.
30. And it's encouraging frustrated educators to leave the classroom and launch their own alternatives to school.
31. Homeschooling is all about having the liberty to learn. (Adapted from McDonald, 2019)

As an overarching concept, a political rationale to homeschool takes on a uniquely anti-democratic disposition. Moreover, homeschooling is, primarily, a function of isolation and individualization. Homeschooling parents want to isolate their children against what they see as "conflicting cultural values" (Bartholet, 2019, p. 9)

One small, but notable, aside of the homeschooling for political rationales includes school funding. Specifically, there are many efforts by those who homeschool to lobby for state-based policies that provide homeschooling families some type of funding for their choice. These homeschooling vouchers or tax credits are designed to provide funding (directly or indirectly) to families who homeschool. Similar to a school voucher that provides government funding to families to send their children to private schools, similar policies that provide funding for homeschooling families redirect tax dollars away from public schools to support homeschoolers. In the event that the funding exceeds the individual family's tax contribution, the additional funds are paid for by other citizens. For vouchers, as was the case in 2016, the average cost to educate a student in Georgia was $9,769. Providing the full amount to be used as a publicly-funded subsidy to offset the cost of private school tuition would require tax money paid by approximately six to seven other families as the median property tax paid by Georgians (and where the bulk of education funding derives) was $1,346. At present, there are only three states that provide state public tax payer money to support private homeschooling: Illinois, Louisiana, and Minnesota (Southeast Homeschool Expo, n.d.).

While some families homeschool out of explicit political ideologies (see, for example, Westover, 2018), the religious orientation of many Protestant Evangelical Christians are interwoven with political aims and dispositions. As noted in the previous chapter, the aim of many religious homeschooling families is to simultaneously protect their children from the interpreted evils of secular public school but also to "train up" a future generation that will expand the role of this narrow Christianity throughout public schools and government. An example of this religion/politics partnership is the Ron Paul Curriculum. Paul, a notoriously libertarian U.S. Congressman whose son, Rand Paul carries on in his legacy, is staunchly anti-government despite being, in effect, a government employee. The Ron Paul Curriculum is "a homeschooling program with an emphasis on 'the Biblical principal of self-government and personal responsibility which is also the foundation of the free market economy'" (Stewart, 2019, p. 119). This religious and political partnership aims to "get busy in constructing a Bible-based social, political, and religious order which finally denies the religious liberty of the enemies of God" (Stewart, 2019, p. 119). In this view, school curriculum and practices that are not aligned with a specific interpretation of the Bible are considered evil and any type of regulations on unfettered free-market capitalism is understood as going against God. In this logic, as it were, God is a fan of unregulated capitalism, meritocracy where individuals pull themselves up by their own bootstraps, and where any policy, practice, or content knowledge that does not reinforce such narrow political or religious doctrine is classified as "the enemy." Though, not all arguments in favor of homeschooling are overtly religious. Reason – the libertarian magazine – often publishes stories in support of school choice and occasionally holds up homeschooling as an ideal form of schooling that is superior to the "government controlled" public schools (Tuccille, 2019). While the rationales given often echo claims of efficiency and effectiveness like those explicated in Chapters 6 and 7, many times the rationale is simply that any form of schooling – and any form of anything – that is not affiliated with some form of government is preferred for the sake of preferring markets over collective government. Moreover, this political disposition is often wedded to specific religious dogmas as,

> In the drive for homeschooling and the privatization of public education; in the providential history of Christian nation mythologizers; in their insistence that public officials be guided by a "biblical worldview"; in the unabashed commitment to the subordination of women, part of the order and structure of the universe as God intended; in the fusion of the bible with libertarian economics – eve in their arguments for gun rights and against universal health care – today's Christian nationalists follow the logic, if not necessarily the theology, laid down by Rushdoony. (Stewart, 2019, pp. 122–123)

In sum, while not all homeschooling families chose to keep their children at home as a manifestation of their political affinity, many do and such dispositions are often aligned with a very specific religious outlook on policy, practice, curriculum, pedagogy, and society. As Stewart suggested, "what they actually oppose is simply secular, democratic government, whereas what they invariably support is religious or theocratic government" (Stewart, 2019, p. 124). As argued by Cynthia Dunbar (Dunbar, 2008), the homeschooling parent and former Chair of the Texas Board of Education, Christian homeschooling and other forms of school choice are necessary to prevent the spread of liberalism and are vital to establishing the United States as a theocratic government singularly oriented to the Protestant Evangelical worldview.

### References

Bartholet, E. (2019). Homeschooling: Parent rights absolutism vs child rights to education & protection. *Arizona Law Review, 62*(1), 1–80.

Dunbar, C. (2008). *One nation under god: How the left is trying to erase what made us great.* HigherLife Publishing.

Hifalutin Homeschooler. (2018). *10 honest reasons parents choose to homeschool: And the politically correct defense we hide behind.* Retrieved March 1, 2020, from https://hifalutinhomeschooler.com/10-reasons-parents-homeschool/

HSLDA. (n.d.). *Education tax credits.* Retrieved March 28, 2020, from https://hslda.org/content/docs/nche/Issues/T/Tax_Ed_Credits.asp

Lubienski, C., & Brewer, T. J. (2014). Does home education "work"? Challenging the assumptions behind the home education movement. In P. Rothermel (Ed.), *International perspectives on home education: Do we still need schools?* (pp. 136–147). Palgrave.

MacLean, N. (2017). *Democracy in chains: The deep history of the radical right's stealth plan for America*. Penguin Books.

Ray, B. D. (2016). Introduction to recent changes and research in us homeschooling. In B. S. Cooper, F. R. Speilhagen, & C. Ricci (Eds.), *Homeschooling in new view* (2nd ed., pp. 3–28). Information Age Publishing.

Silva, E. (2018). *The state of homeschooling in America.* Retrieved March 30, 2020, from https://psmag.com/education/the-state-of-homeschooling-in-america

Southeast Homeschool Expo. (n.d.). *What can homeschoolers deduct on their taxes?* Retrieved March 1, 2020, from https://www.southeasthomeschoolexpo.com/tax-deduction-for-homeschoolers/

Stewart, K. (2019). *The power worshippers: Inside the dangerous rise of religious nationalism*. Bloomsbury Publishing.

Tuccille, J. D. (2019). *Homeschooling produces better-educated, more-tolerant kids. Politicians hate that.* Retrieved February 17, 2020, from https://reason.com/2019/01/22/homeschooling-produces-better-students/

Westover, T. (2018). *Educated: A memoir*. Random House.

CHAPTER 5

# Claims of Effectiveness

Within the pro-homeschooling landscape there is quite a bit of promotion and fanfare surrounding claims that homeschooling, itself as a treatment, provides an environment that is more conducive to better academic outcomes and, as a result, produces better academic outcomes as compared to those of local public schools. For example,

> Studies on the academic achievement of homeschoolers continue to demonstrate that they consistently score at or above average on standardized tests. In a 2009 study of standardized academic achievement tests (conducted by Brian Ray, PhD, with the NHERI), homeschooled children averaged at or above the eightieth percentile. The national average for traditionally schooled children on standardized tests is the fiftieth percentile. (Linsenbach, 2010, p. 28)

Similarly, the following is a filtered list of the "100 Reasons to Homeschool Your Kids" that relate to claims of effectiveness.

1. Homeschoolers perform well academically.
2. Whether early, late, or somewhere in the middle, homeschooling allows all children to move at their own pace.
3. You can choose from a panoply of curriculum options based on your children's needs and your family's educational philosophy.
4. Or you can focus on unschooling, a self-directed education approach tied to a child's interests.
5. Homeschooling gives your kids plenty of time to play! In a culture where childhood free play is disappearing, preserving play is crucial to a child's health and well-being.
6. They can have more recess and less homework.
7. You can take advantage of weekly homeschool park days, field trips, classes, and other gatherings offered through a homeschooling group near you.
8. Homeschooling co-ops are growing, so you can find support and resources.

© KONINKLIJKE BRILL NV, LEIDEN, 2021 | DOI: 10.1163/9789004457096_005

9. Homeschooling learning centers are sprouting worldwide, prioritizing self-directed education and allowing more flexibility to more families who want to homeschool.

10. Parks, beaches, libraries, and museums are often less crowded during school hours, and many offer programming specifically for homeschoolers.

11. More urban parents are choosing to homeschool, prioritizing family and individualized learning.

12. Your kids' summertime can be fully self-directed, as can the rest of their year.

13. That's because kids thrive under self-directed education.

14. Your kids don't have to wait for adulthood to pursue their passions.

15. Self-directed learning centers for teen homeschoolers can provide a launchpad for community college classes and jobs while offering peer connection and adult mentoring.

16. You can preserve their natural childhood creativity.

17. Schools kill creativity, as Sir Ken Robinson proclaims in his TED Talk, the most-watched one ever.

18. Homeschooling might even help your kids use their creativity in remarkable ways, as other well-known homeschoolers have done.

19. With homeschooling, learning happens all the time, all year round. There are no arbitrary starts and stops.

20. You can take vacations at any time of the year without needing permission from the principal.

21. Or you can go world-schooling, spending extended periods of time traveling the world together as a family or letting your teens travel the world without you.

22. Technological innovations make self-education through homeschooling not only possible but also preferable.

23. Free, online learning programs like Khan Academy, Duolingo, Scratch, Prodigy Math, and MIT OpenCourseWare complement learning in an array of topics, while others, like Lynda.com and Mango, may be available for free through your local public library.

24. Teen homeschoolers can enroll in an online high school program to earn a high school diploma if they choose.

25. But young people don't need a high school diploma in order to go to college.

26. Many teen homeschoolers take community college classes and transfer into four-year universities with significant credits and cost-savings.

Research suggests that community college transfers also do better than their non-transfer peers.

27. Homeschooling may be the new path to Harvard.
28. Many colleges openly recruit and welcome homeschoolers because they tend to be "innovative thinkers."
29. Hybrid homeschooling models are popping up everywhere, allowing more families access to this educational option.
30. Homeschooling grants children remarkable freedom and autonomy, particularly self-directed approaches like unschooling, but it's definitely not the *Lord of the Flies*.
31. Homeschooling allows for much more authentic, purposeful learning tied to interests and everyday interactions in the community rather than contrived assignments at school.
32. Homeschooling can be preferable to school because it's a totally different learning environment. As homeschooling pioneer John Holt wrote in *Teach Your Own*: "What is most important and valuable about the home as a base for children's growth in the world is not that it is a better school than the schools but that it isn't a school at all."
33. Immersed in their larger community and engaged in genuine, multi-generational activities, homeschoolers tend to be better socialized than their schooled peers. Newer studies suggest the same.
34. Homeschoolers interact daily with an assortment of people in their community in pursuit of common interests, not in an age-segregated classroom with a handful of teachers.
35. They can dig deeper into emerging passions, becoming highly proficient.
36. They also have the freedom to quit.
37. They can spend abundant time outside and in nature. (Adapted from McDonald, 2019)

Of the myriad of rationales and justifications for homeschooling, the claim of effectiveness is among the most cited reason. The majority of the claims about effectiveness are largely overstated. That is, while homeschooled students do, on average, perform at or above the academic levels of their traditional public school counterparts, there is little evidence that homeschooling – as a treatment – is responsible for the outcomes as other factors such as family socioeconomic status likely play a larger determining factor. As such, students who are homeschooled and enter/exit traditional public schools tend to maintain their higher level of academic achievement suggesting greater causality of other out-of-school factors rather than the treatment itself.

On the face of it these claims are accurate but are exceedingly problematic for a number of reasons. Namely among those reasons are the comparison groups themselves as it is an apples to oranges comparison when the full context is understood.

Comparing student academic outcomes has long been a quest within the commodified and quantified era of accountability. Moreover, the comparison of a student's performance to their peer's performance is in alignment with our broad societal commitment to the myth of meritocracy where such comparisons are required to determine the worth and value of a human within our capitalistic economy. As education is understood, widely, as a level playing field despite the myriad reasons it should not be understood as one, the relative difference or variance between student academic performance purports to tell us something about the student and the quality of the school in which she attends. Following the logic, as it were, is that a singular student who does well relative to her peers is the result of hard work. The collective average of student academic performance at School A relative to the performance of the average student performance of students at School B purport to tell us about the relative difference in overall quality of the schools. If, say, the average SAT score of students at School B is 20% higher than the average score of students at School A, then conclusions are often drawn about School B "producing" better students or providing better educational experiences that lead to such outcomes while School A is understood to be "failing" or lacking in some way. Within the broader push to privatize and monetize schools, reformers would call for School A to be converted into a charter school, converted into a "turnaround" school, provide students with vouchers to attend private schools, or transfer to School B. All of these proposed options would result in fewer funds for School A, an exodus of students who come from families with the financial means to enact school choice decisions, thus leaving School A with a higher concentration of lower-performing students from less affluent families, thus driving scores down and becoming further proof of the "failure" and need to privatize in some way. And, yet, comparing a singular student in either School A or B with another student in the same school, or the other, is fraught with problems. Decades of research have concluded, definitively, that out-of-school factors inform two-thirds of all variance between student academic outcomes (Berliner, 2006, 2013; Berliner & Biddle, 1995; Berliner & Glass, 2014; Bowles & Gintis, 1976; Brewer & Myers, 2015; Carter & Welner, 2013; Coleman, 1990; Coleman et al., 1966; Ennis, 1976; Jencks & Phillips, 1998; Jencks et al., 1972; Ladson-Billings, 2006; Rothstein, 2004; Wilkinson & Pickett, 2010) . One-third of the variance can be explained by in-school factors. With this understanding, it becomes clearer that comparing the academic performance of students even within the same school is not as clear-cut as reformers would have us believe as the vast majority of the variance is not explained by the school itself and, thus, conclusions and policy prescriptions that rely on assuming that it is the school – as a treatment – are misguided.

With that in mind, comparisons of the academic outcomes of students who are homeschooled to those who attend public schools is ever more problematic. Comparing the average SAT scores (Linsenbach, 2010), grades, test scores, graduation rate, and college acceptance/competition rates of homeschooled students with the average of public school students requires ignoring the glaring contextual differences between the typical homeschooled student and the typical student attending public schools. As will be explicated in greater detail in the following chapter, the median household income for American families in 2019 was approximately $63,000 while the median household income for families that homeschooled during the same year was approximately $94,000. The role that a family's socioeconomic status has on informing student academic outcomes has been fully documented over a nearly seventy year period of time.

A student's socioeconomic (SES) status is historically the most prominently considered factor (though, as will be explicated below, the SES factor is closely related to racial factors in U.S. history). Family SES is the leading factor when predicting all forms of social and economic inequality in the U.S. – including educational opportunity and educational outcomes.

Evidence suggests that "the influence of social class characteristics is probably so powerful that schools cannot overcome it, no matter how well trained are their teachers and no matter how well designed are their instructional programs and climates" (Rothstein, 2004, p. 5). Further, "the spatial concentration of affluence and poverty in rich and poor school districts raises the odds that affluent children will receive a superior education and that poor children will get inferior schooling, virtually guaranteeing the intergenerational transmission of class position" (Massey, 2007, p. 197). Rothstein further points out that children from lower SES deciles are exposed to "more lead poisoning, more asthma, poorer nutrition, less adequate pediatric care, more exposure to smoke, and a host of other problems" (Rothstein, 2004, p. 3) when compared to students from higher SES deciles. Indeed, when measuring student educational outcomes, it becomes clear that the leading factor in determining and predicting educational outcomes rests almost singularly with a student's SES. That is, regardless of where students score on early tests, SES factors have such a powerful influence on results that, over time, higher scoring students from low SES families are surpassed by their initially lower scoring but higher SES peers. With connections to the argument set forth by Bowles and Gintis (1976), Paul Willis' work reinforces the evidence that a schools' function is to reproduce class stratification – in the case of Willis' young men who reproduced their class by way of opposition of the cultures of the ruling elite, the provision of an equal education for them would have caused menial labor employers to "strugg[le] to press [the boys] into meaningless work" (Willis, 1977, p. 177). That is, work that is associated with low wages and the working class.

Because we know from decades of research that a family's socioeconomic status is the key indicator of informing academic outcomes, it should be of little surprise that homeschooled students generally do better than their public school counterparts. This is not a result of the homeschooling itself, it is simply a result of coming from more money. Comparatively, private schools generally outperform public schools on the NAEP each year. However, when controlling for economic factors by comparing the scores of similarly wealthy families who attend public schools, the students in the public schools far outperform their private school counterparts who share similar home economic realities (Lubienski & Lubienski, 2014).

Reports of academic outcomes at a local public school entail a myriad of factors that provide both an overarching snapshot of the academic environment but also numerous snapshots and disaggregated data between a plethora of testing and the type(s) of students taking those assessments. I do, up front, want to be clear that I am not taking a position of support for the status quo of the assessment practices and hyper-accountability culture within traditional public schools. There is much to be explored and said about how these environments can be negative to both the culture of education and, in some cases, individual students or student groups and such conversations are wholly worthwhile (see, for example, Ahlquist, 2011; Baker, 2011; Berliner, 2006, 2013; Darling-Hammond, 2012; Glass, 2008; Goldstein, 2014; Haertel, 2013; Hursh, 2011; Jencks & Phillips, 1998; Kumashiro, 2015; Labaree, 2012; Lack, 2011; Mathis, 2013; Newman & Chin, 2003; Olsen, 2015; Peterson et al., 2011; Ravitch, 2010; Willis & Sandholtz, 2009). That said, what I am interested in here is a discussion of the fallacies of comparing the academic outcomes of students who are homeschooled to those of students in public schools.

There are a variety of ways to measure academic achievement or academic outcomes. In normal usage, discussions surrounding achievement typically refer to student test scores and/or student GPAs in some cases (which are derived from a student's overall scores within and across their course-specific assessments). Academic outcomes, on the other hand, often refer to student graduation rates, drop-out rates, college acceptance rates, college matriculation rates, and college completion rates. In some ways, what is measured as an outcome can be thought of in terms of what the tangible outcomes of schooling and education can, or should, produce. Academic achievement – again, not without some important caveats that should be considered – is more a measurement of the transactional events within the schooling and education process and often a singular glimpse – or gauge of temperature by way of a metaphor – of a particular moment in time. While some of these achievement metrics are somewhat cumulative in nature (think, for example, a high school graduation test that purports to assess the content knowledge learned over the course of four years of study), as a function of the limitations of testing, they still provide a singular glimpse into what we might call learning. That is, the test scores of a student taking a high school graduation test may very well be influenced by external factors such as sleep, hunger, student volition during the day of the exam, temperature in the room, etc., and should be understood within such possible limitations.

One of the largest claims of homeschooling effectiveness relative to public schools is its ability to provide individualized learning or "personalized learning" in ways that are not, apparently, possible in group settings. There, again, are some issues here with the delivery method and the person delivering the treatment. While more individualized learning approaches have benefits (also noting that this can be, and is done, in public K-12 schools) this approach as a treatment, alone, may not be sufficient nor appropriate depending on how it is delivered and who is doing the delivery. To return to a medical analogy, an individualized plan of surgery and subsequent individualized course of antibiotics and medicines that take the individual's heath history and contemporary medical concerns into consideration and individualized physical therapy are, with little doubt, the best way to approach most medical procedures. That is, individualized to the patient's needs and speed of recovery. However, while this process is ideally individualized, if the individual overseeing the surgery, administration of medicine, and facilitating the physical therapy is not a licensed and trained medical professional, then the best individualized healthcare plan is worthless. Moreover, the increased access to a myriad of technology and YouTube videos, would not make such an individual more suited to provide such medical intervention. Despite all of this, many homeschooling families claim that parents are the best suited facilitator of this individualized approach to learning despite having any training, credentialing, or licensure at providing such pedagogical experiences. In fact, it is entirely feasible that the advent on-demand echo chamber inducing technologies may prove to negatively reinforce many of these approaches (Bryant, 2020). In our over-the-top societal praise of billionaires and tech-gurus, Business Insider has even pushed homeschooling as an ideal educational delivery method because "Bill Gates and Mark Zuckerberg are big fans of personalized learning, since it tends to use technology as a way to tailor lesson plans to students" (Weller, 2018). Nowhere in the article was it pointed out that two tech industry giants who rely on the sales and use of technology to bolster their fortunes would, of course, be in favor of expanding the reach of technology.

Returning to the problem at hand of comparing the academic achievements and academic outcomes of homeschooled students to those of students in public schools is, again, presents a problem in comparison groups. All of the factors explicated above in terms of academic achievement and academic outcomes reported by a local public school or school district are reported as averages or medians of hundreds, if not thousands, of students. Thus, on its face, comparing the academic achievements and outcomes of, say, a singular homeschooled student to the average or median of thousands of public school students is statistical malfeasance. While individual students (in both homeschooling and public schooling environments) can compare their individual scores and outcomes to the larger group median or average, few concluding generalizations can, or should, be drawn about the comparative experiences.

Another problematic function of the comparison of a small group of homeschooled students to those of the millions of public school students is that because public schools operate within, and under, the oversight of local, state, and federal accountability, all student metrics associated with achievement and outcomes are reported. As Bartholet (2019) points out, because not all homeschooled students are required to even notify the State about their decision to homeschool, it raises significant questions about comparing the self-reported metrics from homeschooled students to all public school students. That is,

> Studies which make claims about homeschoolers' performance capture only those who are most visible because they emerge from isolation to do things like take standardized tests, apply to college, or attend college. If, as is often the case, parents are in charge of test administration, they may only submit test results or reveal them to researchers if they are positive, either for friar of state intervention, or because researchers are often only looking for positive results. This means studies generally focus on a small subset of the most successful homeschoolers, and miss out entirely on the most at-risk [or lower performing] subsets. (Bartholet, 2019, p. 16)

And, as was noted previously, what we "know" about homeschooling families tends to be limited as their participation in Department of Education surveys is the lowest participation rate of all groups surveyed.

While the effects of poverty and lower SES can create similar barriers to equal educational opportunities and outcomes for those who experience such factors, racial inequality often exacerbates those effects of SES. Namely, race is a dominant factor alone but is often correlated with SES factors in the US given the nation's abhorrent history of racial relations between Whites and non-Whites. That is, a Black student, for example, is far more likely to experience poverty in the US than a White student and subsequently attend a school that receives less financing than a predominately White school (Jencks et al., 1972). As a result, while racial factors are important considerations, they can become magnified through the experience of economic inequality. For example, "in recent decades, [B]lacks have experienced substantially less upward intergenerational mobility and substantially more downward intergenerational mobility than [W]hites" (Mazumder, 2014, p. 2). Pauline Lipman contends, that the "correlation between poverty and low-academic performance, school completion, and other education indicators [is] well-documented, as is the relationship between race/ethnicity and educational outcomes" (Lipman, 2011, p. 79), even within efforts to improve opportunity based on "mixed-income" schooling, the actual "subtext is race" (Lipman, 2011, p. 75).

So, what does all of this mean for comparisons of academic outcomes between homeschooled students and those who attend public schools? While children who are homeschooled often outperform their public school counterparts the difference, simply put, can be attributed to the massive disparity in family income and what that income can, and does, mean for educational opportunities, educative experiences, access to technology, books, trips, etc. and to a great extent, an overall lack of detailed and transparent reporting from families who homeschool.

### References

Ahlquist, R. (2011). The 'empire' strikes back via a neoliberal agenda: Confronting the legacies of colonialism. In R. Ahlquist, P. C. Gorski, & T. Montano (Eds.), *Assault on kids: How hyper-accountability, corporatization, deficit ideologies, and Ruby Payne are destroying our schools* (pp. 9–32). Peter Lang Publishing.

Baker, K. (2011, Spring). High test scores: The wrong road to national economic success. *Kappa Delta Pi Record, 47*, 116–120.

Bartholet, E. (2019). Homeschooling: Parent rights absolutism vs child rights to education & protection. *Arizona Law Review, 62*(1), 1–80.

Berliner, D. C. (2006). Our impoverished view of educational reform. *Teachers College Record, 108*, 949–995.

Berliner, D. C. (2013). Effects of inequality and poverty vs. Teachers and schooling on America's youth. *Teachers College Record, 115*, 1–26.

Berliner, D. C., & Biddle, B. J. (1995). *The manufactured crisis: Myths, fraud, and the attack on America's public schools*. Addison-Wesley.

Berliner, D. C., & Glass, G. V. (2014). *50 myths and lies that threaten America's public schools: The real crisis in education*. Teachers College Press.

Bowles, S., & Gintis, H. (1976). *Schooling in capitalist America*. Harper Collins.

Brewer, T. J., & Myers, P. S. (2015). How neoliberalism subverts equality and perpetuates poverty in our nation's schools. In S. N. Haymes, M. V. d. Haymes, & R. Miller (Eds.), *The routledge handbook of poverty in the United States* (pp. 190–198). Routledge.

Bryant, J. (2020). *Homeschooling movement sees opportunity during health calamity*. Retrieved April 7, 2020, from https://www.laprogressive.com/homeschooling-movement/

Carter, P. L., & Welner, K. G. (Eds.). (2013). *Closing the opportunity gap: What America must do to give every child and even chance*. Oxford University Press.

Coleman, J. (1990). *Equality and achievement in education*. Westview Press.

Coleman, J., Campbell, E. Q., Hobson, C. J., McPartland, J., Mood, A. M., Weinfeld, F. D., & York, R. L. (1966). *Equality of educational opportunity*. U.S. Department of Health, Education, and Welfare.

Darling-Hammond, L. (2012). Value-added teacher evaluation: The harm behind the hype. *Education Week, 31*(24), 32–24.

Ennis, R. H. (1976). Equality of educational opportunity. *Educational Theory, 26*(1), 3–18.

Glass, G. V. (2008). *Fertilizers, pills, and magnet strips: The fate of public education in America*. Information Age Publishing.

Goldstein, D. (2014). *The teacher wars: A history of America's most embattled profession*. Doubleday.

Haertel, E. H. (2013). *Reliability and validity of inferences about teachers based on student test scores*. ETS. https://www.ets.org/Media/Research/pdf/PICANG14.pdf

Hursh, D. (2011). The Gates Foundation's interventions into educaiton, health, and food policies: Technology, power, and the privatization of political problems. In P. E. Kovacs (Ed.), *The Gates foundation and the future of U.S. "public" schools* (pp. 39–52). Routledge.

Jencks, C., & Phillips, M. (Eds.). (1998). *The Black-White test score gap*. Brookings Institution Press.

Jencks, C., Smith, M., Acland, H., Bane, M. J., Cohen, D., Gintis, H., … Michelson, S. (1972). *Inequality: A reassessment of the effect of family and schooling in America*. Basic Books, Inc.

Kumashiro, K. (2015). *Review of proposed 2015 federal teacher preparation regulations*. National Education Policy Center. http://nepc.colorado.edu/thinktank/review-proposed-teacher-preparation

Labaree, D. (2012). The lure of statistics for educational researchers. In P. Smeyers & M. Depaepe (Eds.), *Educational research: The ethics and aesthetics of statistics* (pp. 13–25). Springer.

Lack, B. (2011). Anti-democratic militaristic education: An overview and critical analysis of KIPP schools. In R. Ahlquist, P. C. Gorski, & T. Montano (Eds.), *Assault on kids: How hyper-accountability, corporatization, deficit ideologies, and Ruby Payne are destroying our schools* (pp. 65–90). Peter Lang Publishing.

Ladson-Billings, G. (2006). From the achievement gap to the education debt: Understanding achievement in U.S. schools. *Educational Researcher, 35*(7), 3–12.

Linsenbach, S. (2010). *The everything guide to homeschooling: All you need too create the best curriculum and learning environment for your child.* Adams Media.

Lipman, P. (2011). *The new political economy of urban education: Neoliberalism, race, and the right to the city.* Routledge.

Lubienski, C., & Lubienski, S. (2014). *The public school advantage: Why public schools outperform private schools.* The University of Chicago Press.

Massey, D. S. (2007). *Categorically unequal: The American stratification system.* Russell Sage Foundation.

Mathis, W. (2013). *Research-based options for education policymaking.* National Education Policy Center. http://nepc.colorado.edu/publication/options

Mazumder, B. (2014). *Black-White differences in intergenerational economic mobility in the United States.* Federal Reserve Bank of Chicago.

McDonald, K. (2019). *100 reasons to homeschool your kids.* Retrieved July 8, 2019, from https://fee.org/articles/100-reasons-to-homeschool-your-kids/

Newman, K. S., & Chin, M. M. (2003). High stakes: Time poverty, testing, and the children of the working poor. *Qualitative Sociology, 26*(1), 3–34.

Olsen, R. (2015). *The toxic myth of good and bad teachers.* Retrieved January 16, 2017, from https://www.richardolsen.me/b/2015/05/the-toxic-myth-of-good-and-bad-teachers/

Peterson, E. R., Rubie-Davies, C. M., Elley-Brown, M. J., Widdowson, D. A., Dixon, R. S., & Irving, S. E. (2011). Who is to blame? Students, teachers and parents views on who is responsible for student achievement. *Research in Education, 86*(1), 1–12.

Ravitch, D. (2010). *The death and life of the great American school system: How testing and choice are undermining education.* Basic Books.

Rothstein, R. (2004). *Class and schools: Using social, economic, and educational reform to close the Black-White achievement gap.* Economic Policy Institute.

Weller, C. (2018). *Homeschooling could be the smartest way to teach kids in the 21st century – Here are 5 reasons why.* Retrieved April 1, 2020, from https://www.businessinsider.com/reasons-homeschooling-is-the-smartest-way-to-teach-kids-today-2018-1

Wilkinson, R., & Pickett, K. (2010). *The spirit level: Why greater equality makes societies stronger.* Bloomsbury Press.

Willis, J., & Sandholtz, J. (2009). Constrained professionalism: Dilemmas of teaching in the face of test-based accountability. *Teachers College Record, 111*(4), 1065–1114.

Willis, P. (1977). *Learning to labor: How working class kids get working class jobs.* Columbia University Press.

CHAPTER 6

# Claims of Efficiency

Efficiency is a question of relativity. If outputs are able to be increased at the same, or preferably lower, costs then the level of efficiency is increased. If X product can solve the same, or more, problems than Y product and it costs less to produce and maintain X, then X is said to be more efficient. The question of efficiency with homeschooling follows the claims that homeschooling outperforms public schools. This claim must be understood and accepted first before claims of efficiency can be made. And, as explicated in the previous chapter, claims of outcomes of homeschooling relative to public schools are tenuous, at best, and misleading at worst. Yet, for a moment, we will take up the assumption pushed by homeschooling advocates that the outcomes of homeschooling compared to public schools is an apples to apples comparison and, thus, evaluations of relative costs (and therefore efficiency) can be considered.

According to the National Center for Education Statistics, the total expenditure for students in the United States during the 2015–2016 school year was $706 billion which equated to $13,847 per student ($12,330 for educational expenses such as teacher salary, employee benefits, supplies, etc. and $1,155 for capital outlays such as buildings and infrastructure) (NCES, n.d.). The bulk of public school expenditures go to cover the salaries of teachers, principals, administrators, and other support staff. Yet, it is important to keep in mind that this is a raw average as the actual per-student expenditure varies dramatically across states and even by district. In 2016, Utah spent only $6,953 per student while New York spent $22,366 with a median expense of $11,390 (Governing, n.d.). The variation in spending per student is based largely on cost of living differences but can also reflect political attitudes towards governmental spending. Comparatively, homeschooling advocates suggest that it only costs about $500 to educate a child at home annually (Bentley, n.d.-a).

The HSLDA provides a detailed breakdown of the projected costs of homeschooling noting that curriculum is the largest expense but can vary depending on thrift. Costs associated with curriculum can be offset by taking advantage of local libraries and YouTube videos. Combining back-of-the-napkin calculations for a myriad of expenses including curriculum, professional memberships (one with HSLDA, of course), annual homeschooling convention, school supplies, etc. the cost to homeschool three children would be $2,275 or $758 per child (Bentley, n.d.-b). However, when considering the costs of educating a child, the HSLDA provides the following caveat: "last, but certainly not least,

© KONINKLIJKE BRILL NV, LEIDEN, 2021 | DOI: 10.1163/9789004457096_006

pray about the needs you have for your homeschool and ask God to provide these things" (Bentley, n.d.-b). To the task of determining and comparing efficiencies between homeschooling and public schools, it is decidedly difficult to quantify the value of those resources provided by God for comparative purposes.

Within the broader libertarian and neoliberal critique of government-run traditional public schools is that government, itself, is terribly inefficient at running, overseeing, and providing services generally speaking. The logic, as it were, is that the additional levels of bureaucracy associated with governments that are in place to ensure accountability and oversight create unnecessary burdens on the delivery of goods and services and, thus, add unnecessary costs. Rather than operating under such a system, pro-market ideologies assert that free-markets and deregulation (both understood as being connected and equally separate concepts and practices) will turn over the services long managed by governments to the invisible hand of the free market and, as a result, will force such services to adapt to the efficiencies that are believed to come with market competition as opposed to government monopolies.

Beginning heavily in the 1980s, the education policy landscape has seen increased efforts to deregulate schools and teacher preparation by turning them over to free market oriented reforms. The push to deregulate schools has been a result of not only this generic political and economic ideology that market competition is always preferred over government-run services but it has been bolstered by the continued myth of the 'failed public school' and the 'bad teacher.' It is important, now, to point out that the critique of efforts to reform and privatize education that follows should not be understood or interpreted as an endorsement of the status quo or the history of public schools. Indeed, public schools have been wrought with inequalities and injustices – primarily centering around issues of race and class – and this is a troubled history that warrants critique and reform. That said, the inequalities within public schools have long been a mirror of the inequalities within the larger society and while schools have long been responsible for the reproduction of such inequalities (Bowles & Gintis, 1976), they are not, singularly, responsible for the creation of such inequity. Ultimately, because schools have long been understood as providing an equal and level playing field within the guise of meritocracy (Brewer & Myers, 2015), the persistence of socioeconomic inequalities has been understood as: (1) a failure of the public school system to ameliorate systemic poverty; and/or, (2) a failure of students and their communities to take advantage of those perceived equal opportunities. Indeed, many homeschooling parents simply want to isolate their children away from those students and communities that are understood through deficit ideologies (Ahlquist, Gorski,

& Montano, 2011; Gorski, 2011). Further, teachers have increasingly become the scapegoat for these perceived failures and, as a result, have become targets of unfair critique (Goldstein, 2014; Kumashiro, 2012). While the myth of the failed school can be traced back to the launch of Sputnik (and the perceived failure of U.S. public schools to produce students capable of competing with the Soviet Union), there has been a heightened sense of critique stemming from the Regan administration's release of *A Nation at Risk* (ANAR) and his administration's embrace of the free-market neoliberal ideologies espoused by Milton Friedman (deMarrais, Brewer, Atkinson, Herron, & Lewis, 2019; Harvey, 2005).

Policy efforts that purport to attend to these perceived failures have manifested by way of charter schools (Lubienski & Weitzel, 2010), school vouchers (Lubienski & Brewer, 2016), alternative teacher certification programs (Brewer, 2014; Brewer & deMarrais, 2015; Brewer, Kretchmar, Sondel, Ishmael, & Manfra, 2016), and a resurgence of homeschooling (Brewer & Lubienski, 2017; Lubienski & Brewer, 2014; Lubienski, Puckett, & Brewer, 2013).

The NHERI claims that homeschooling families save taxpayers over $27 billion per year because taxpayers spend, on average, $11,732 per student per year and the average expenditure to homeschool a student is $600 per student annually (Ray, 2019). On the surface it would appear that Ray is correct that the homeschooling of 2.3 million students at a reduced cost of $11,132 per year ($11,732 – $600) would equate to savings of $25,603,600,000 annually.

However, these figures are wildly misleading on the face of it. The majority of households that homeschool are a two-parent household where only one parent is in the labor force. As such, the majority of homeschooling families forgo a second source of income to stay at home and homeschool.

A survey conducted Brian Ray in 2009 noted that the median income for families who homeschool was $74,049 in 2006 dollars or $78,490 in 2008 dollars, controlling for inflation (Ray, 2009b). Updating those numbers to 2019 suggests that the estimation of comparative dollars would be $94,083 (U.S. Inflation Calculator, n.d.). Estimates of the national median of household income in the United States during 2019 hover around $63,000 (Seeking Alpha, 2019). Thus, the typical homeschooling family makes nearly 50% more than the typical household in the United States. And this is a striking and notable reality considering that the majority of homeschooling families have willingly forgone a parent's salary so that they can remain at home to teach their children. And while this is certainly not the case in all iterations of homeschooling, a single-income that is 50% larger than the national median *household* income positions the earner themselves at the top of the individual-earning bracket. The FRED data suggests that the real median personal income in 2016 was $31,099 (FRED, n.d.) or $33,189 adjusted to 2019 dollars (U.S. Inflation

Calculator, n.d.). With this in mind, it becomes clearer that the claims made by the NHERI and other homeschooling advocacy organizations and individuals that the cost of homeschooling is significantly less than the collective cost of sending a child to a traditional public school fall flat on their face. Claiming that it only costs $600 per year to homeschool a child requires some convenient assumptions and omissions by homeschooling advocates: (1) That there would be enough household income to offset the loss of an income stream from the person staying home to teach – traditionally, but not always, the mother; (2) That there are additional costs associated with 2+ people staying at home for the majority of the day (e.g., heating and air conditioning, electricity, etc.) when compared to a house that might normally be vacant during the day; (3) shifts the funding accountability of what is normally understood as a public good to the individual; (4) that the suggested weekly outings and fieldtrips would equate to increased – but not reported – costs related to transportation and entry fees (e.g., museum admission); and, (4) fails to recognize that the public is still providing some funding and services towards a child's education through the collective funding of public libraries, roads, facilities and materials for extracurricular activities organized by a traditional public school and made available to homeschoolers, etc.

So, not only does the median homeschooling household make upwards of 50% more than the median household in the United States, if the household income of a homeschooling family is the result of a single-income (again, assuming that one parent is not working to stay at home to conduct homeschooling), then it is suggestive that the typical single-income of a homeschooling household is three times the national median. Said another way, a single-income of a homeschooling family may bring in the equivalent of what three other Americans make in their jobs ($33,000 compared to $94,000). Comparisons of the academic outcomes of homeschooled students to their traditional public school counterparts are, therefore, a comparison of apples and oranges. Not only does this apples and oranges comparison grossly misstate the costs associated with homeschooling which are nearly three times the cost, but it hides some of the socioeconomic privileges that are borne out by growing up in a family with considerable relative wealth. We have known for more than half a century that one of the strongest predictors of academic outcomes is a family's socioeconomic status and the resources such wealth can bring – or a lack of resources in the case of relative poverty (Bowles & Gintis, 1976; Brewer & Myers, 2015; Carter & Welner, 2013; Coleman, 1990; Coleman et al., 1966; Ennis, 1976; Jencks & Phillips, 1998; Jencks et al., 1972; Ladson-Billings, 2006; Rothstein, 2004; Wilkinson & Pickett, 2010).

CLAIMS OF EFFICIENCY

TABLE 6.1    Income and educational expenses (in 2019 dollars)

|  | National median | Homeschooling family |
| --- | --- | --- |
| Personal income (singular income) | $33,000 | $94,000[a] |
| Household income (1+ incomes) | $63,000 | $94,000 |
| Reported cost of education | $11,132 | $600 |
| Estimated actual cost of education | $12,251[b] | $33,600[c] |

a  Assumes a single-income household.
b  Includes the estimated $519 in back-to-school spending (Jones, 2019).
c  Estimation combines NHERI homeschooling costs with the median personal income as a forgone income.

These claims of efficiency are similar to the claims made by pro-voucher advocacy organizations and individuals who have suggested that the use of vouchers to allow students to use public funds to offset the costs of private school tuition results in a net savings for tax payers. For example, a report by the pro-voucher organization of EdChoice (which was formerly known as the Friedman Foundation named after Milton Friedman), claimed that,

> In nearly every school choice program, the dollar value of the voucher or scholarship is less than or equal to the state's formula spending per student. This means states are spending the same amount or less on students in school choice programs than they would have spent on the same students if they had attended public schools, producing a fiscal savings. (Aud, 2007, p. 5)

The problem, here, is that while a voucher (or a homeschool tax credit or something similar) that is less than what the state is spending per student for public school attendance gives the appearance of fiscal savings, it disguises the full and hidden costs. That is, in the case of a voucher to attend a private school that is less than the surface costs of the same student attending a public school, the hidden costs are still present and become the burden of both the individual family and for the community. Because most private schools do not provide transportation, it is entirely the financial burden of individual families to arrange for private transportation to attend the private school of their choice. This, obviously, costs money related to the ownership of reliable private transportation (e.g., the car itself, insurance, maintenance, gas, etc.). So, as EdChoice suggests, "If a state spends $6,000 per student in public schools and offers a $5,000 voucher, every student who uses a voucher saves the state $1,000" (Aud, 2007, p. 14). However, the state is, in essence, not saving this full amount (in fact, it increases the cost per student) and the cost burden is shifted to individual families – two realities worth exploring at length.

While EdChoice's surface level math would seem to support claims that school choice mechanisms are efficient because they save the government money, such claims miss the larger picture. While it is true that the removal of a singular student into a homeschooling or private school environment will be one less student utilizing some of the school's resources, the cost of each of those resources understood as a per-student basis goes up. The cost to operate a school bus, air condition a school building, purchase paper towels, etc. generally remain steady despite the total number of students. The total cost to operate a school bus is about the same for 50 students as it is for 10 students. However, the more students that school bus serves, the lower the per-student cost is for the district. Moreover, as school choice mechanisms such as homeschool tax credits or private school vouchers shift money from the hands of the public into private hands, the public school is forced to operate these resources and services not only at a higher per-student cost but with a reduced overall budget as the money changes hands.

Considering the hypothetical math from EdChoice provided above, individual families utilizing a voucher appear to save the state $1,000 through their use of a voucher. However, the use of such a voucher dramatically shifts the financial burden of education to the individual family. Not only are they far more likely to have to supplement the cost of private school tuition above the level that a $5,000 voucher would cover (thus increasing the total cost of education relative to public schools) but they also have to provide their own transportation and in some cases provide volunteer hours.

Aside from the math surrounding the use of publicly-funded school-choice mechanisms, the larger philosophical question here remains about for whom, and by whom, is the purpose of education. The use of tax-credits for homeschooling or vouchers for private school attendance, shifts a significant portion of the funding burden to the individual family which, understanding money as a proxy for values, situates schooling as a process and an ends exclusively for individual purposes. It is the "I got mine, go get your own" mantra manifested in education.

To put it plainly, claims that homeschooling costs less than the cost of educating a child at a local public school are wholly unfounded and misleading. On the surface, claims related to the cost of educating a child are often presented as X expenditures related to curriculum costs compared to Y costs associated with the entire cost of educating a child at a public school. What is often presented is a glaring disparity in the associated costs, presenting home-schooling as an option that not only realizes considerable academic success but does so at a fraction of the cost. If homeschooling does, in fact, produce greater academic outcomes than public schools and it is a function of the type of schooling, *and* it is done considerably cheaper, such a practice is open to the adoption of a commonsensical rhetoric that purports to support home-schooling *over* public schooling. Of course, considerable questions should be raised when there are claims of, or the appearance of, the type of school (e.g., homeschooling) is the mechanism causing the difference in academic outcomes rather than, say, family socioeconomic status, parental educational attainment, etc. Such nuance and context is rarely included in conversations in the pro-homeschooling movement. For instance, the NHERI has a long his-tory of presenting the costs of homeschooling compared to the cost of public schooling in what appears to be an apples to apples comparison but is decid-edly an apples to oranges comparison on deeper examination.

TABLE 6.2    Cost over time

|      | Homeschooling | Public school |
| --- | --- | --- |
| 1999 | $546 | $5,325 |
| 2009 | $400–$599 | $9,963 |
| 2019 | $600 | $11,732 |

SOURCE: ADAPTED FROM RAY (2009A, 2015, 2019)

Note here that the cost associated with educating a child in a local public school has continued to rise over the twenty year period in Table 6.2 whereas the reported costs associated with homeschooling have remained almost entirely flat. The cost associated with educating a child at a state-run public school will, naturally, increase over time as the costs associated with running *any* enterprise becomes more expensive due to inflation. While teacher sala-ries have remained disturbingly low relative to their professional counterparts for the past two decades, there have been necessary raises over time. Costs associated with bussing, electricity, food, etc. have all, likewise, increased over time. But, also, in the decades following the passage of the Individuals with Disabilities Education Act (IDEA), more students are being properly diagnosed with learning disabilities and, as a result of the law, being provided with the necessary accommodations that often bring with them a higher financial cost.

As a society we have committed to providing adequate services for our children who need them and to the varying degree that they need them. This is something to take pride in as a society given that many other countries do not provide these protections and services for all students. That said, the cost per student associated with public education has steadily risen since the passage of IDEA. While anti-public school, pro-privatization, individuals and organizations will claim that slow growth in academic outcomes (which is growth) relative to the faster growing costs is representative of the inefficiency of public education while not acknowledging the impact that IDEA has had on our per-pupil funding. Nevertheless, it should be clear that presenting a rising cost associated with public education while suggesting that the costs associated with homeschooling have remained flat is incredibly deceptive.

On the face of it, homeschooling advocates claim that homeschooled students outperform their public school counterparts for pennies on the dollar, therefore homeschooling represents a more efficient method of education. In fact, the HSLDA has claimed that, "The message is loud and clear. More money does not mean a better education" (Home School Legal Defense Association, 2004). Ray has also claimed that "taxpayers spend nothing on most homeschool students" (Ray, 2015) yet nearly all homeschooling guides, curriculums, and advocates suggest making use of public libraries, public parks, and even the extracurricular options made available by local public schools – thus increasing the actual cost of homeschooling as the funding that makes it possible is omitted from HSLDA calculations.

Ultimately, however, comparisons of homeschooling academic outcomes and those of public schools is not only an apples to oranges comparison (which challenges claims of effectiveness), but when the full financial costs of homeschooling are brought into focus, significant challenges arise to claims of efficiency given the *considerable* amount of money it costs to homeschool. These increased costs include the forgoing of a salary, increased electric costs, increased heating/air costs, increased transportation costs, etc. that are required to teach a child at home.

### References

Ahlquist, R., Gorski, P. C., & Montano, T. (Eds.). (2011). *Assault on kids: How hyper-accountability, corporatization, deficit ideologies, and Ruby Payne are destroying our schools*. Peter Lang Publishing.

Aud, S. L. (2007). *Education by the numbers: The fiscal effect of school choice programs, 1990–2006*. Friedman Foundation. https://www.edchoice.org/wp-content/uploads/2015/09/Education-by-the-Numbers-Fiscal-Effect-of-School-Choice-Programs.pdf

Bentley, V. (n.d.-a). *Homeschooling on a shoestring*. Retrieved April 10, 2020, from https://hslda.org/content/earlyyears/Shoestring.asp

Bentley, V. (n.d.-b). *What does it cost to homeschool?* Retrieved April 10, 2020, from https://hslda.org/content/earlyyears/Costs.asp

Bowles, S., & Gintis, H. (1976). *Schooling in capitalist America*. Harper Collins.

Brewer, T. J. (2014). Accelerated burnout: How teach for America's academic impact model and theoretical framework can foster disillusionment among its corps members. *Educational Studies, 50*(3), 246–263.

Brewer, T. J., & deMarrais, K. (Eds.). (2015). *Teach for America counter-narratives: Alumni speak up and speak out*. Peter Lang.

Brewer, T. J., Kretchmar, K., Sondel, B., Ishmael, S., & Manfra, M. (2016). Teach for America's preferential treatment: School district contracts, hiring decisions, and employment practices. *Educational Evaluation and Policy Analysis, 24*(15), 1–38.

Brewer, T. J., & Lubienski, C. (2017). Homeschooling in the United States: Examining the rationales for individualizing education. *Pro-Posições, 28*(2), 21–38.

Brewer, T. J., & Myers, P. S. (2015). How neoliberalism subverts equality and perpetuates poverty in our nation's schools. In S. N. Haymes, M. V. d. Haymes, & R. Miller (Eds.), *The Routledge handbook of poverty in the United States* (pp. 190–198). Routledge.

Carter, P. L., & Welner, K. G. (Eds.). (2013). *Closing the opportunity gap: What America must do to give every child and even chance*. Oxford University Press.

Coleman, J. (1990). *Equality and achievement in education*. Westview Press.

Coleman, J., Campbell, E. Q., Hobson, C. J., McPartland, J., Mood, A. M., Weinfeld, F. D., & York, R. L. (1966). *Equality of educational opportunity*. U.S. Department of Health, Education, and Welfare.

deMarrais, K., Brewer, T. J., Atkinson, J. C., Herron, B., & Lewis, J. (2019). *Philanthropy, hidden strategy, and collective resistance: A primer for concerned educators*. Myers Education Press.

Ennis, R. H. (1976). Equality of educational opportunity. *Educational Theory, 26*(1), 3–18.

FRED. (n.d.). *Real median personal income in the United States*. https://fred.stlouisfed.org/series/MEPAINUSA672N

Goldstein, D. (2014). *The teacher wars: A history of America's most embattled profession*. Doubleday.

Gorski, P. C. (2011). Thoughts on authenticating the class discourse in education. In R. Ahlquist, P. C. Gorski, & T. Montano (Eds.), *Assault on kids: How hyper-accountability, corporatization, deficit ideologies, and Ruby Payne are destroying our schools* (pp. 152–173). Peter Lang Publishing.

Governing. (n.d.). *Education spending per student by state*. Retrieved April 10, 2020, from https://www.governing.com/gov-data/education-data/state-education-spending-per-pupil-data.html

Harvey, D. (2005). *A brief history of neoliberalism*. Oxford University Press.

Home School Legal Defense Association. (2004). *Academic statistics on homeschooling.* Home School Legal Defense Association. http://www.hslda.org/docs/nche/000010/200410250.asp

Jencks, C., & Phillips, M. (Eds.). (1998). *The Black-White test score gap.* Brookings Institution Press.

Jencks, C., Smith, M., Acland, H., Bane, M. J., Cohen, D., Gintis, H., ... Michelson, S. (1972). *Inequality: A reassessment of the effect of family and schooling in America.* Basic Books, Inc.

Jones, C. (2019). *Don't get sidetracked, carry coupons and focus on price, say back-to-school shoppers.* Retrieved August 5, 2019, from https://www.usatoday.com/story/money/2019/07/10/back-school-shopping-price-sales-what-matter-most/1659567001/

Kumashiro, K. (2012). *Bad teacher! How blaming teachers distorts the bigger picture.* Teachers College Press.

Ladson-Billings, G. (2006). From the achievement gap to the education debt: Understanding achievement in U.S. schools. *Educational Researcher, 35*(7), 3–12.

Linsenbach, S. (2010). *The everything guide to homeschooling: All you need too create the best curriculum and learning environment for your child.* Adams Media.

Lubienski, C., & Brewer, T. J. (2014). Does home education "work"? Challenging the assumptions behind the home education movement. In P. Rothermel (Ed.), *International perspectives on home education: Do we still need schools?* (pp. 136–147). Palgrave.

Lubienski, C., & Brewer, T. J. (2016). An analysis of voucher studies: A closer look at the uses and limitations of 'gold standard' advocacy research. *Peabody Journal of Education, 91*(4), 455–472.

Lubienski, C., Puckett, T., & Brewer, T. J. (2013). Does homeschooling "work"? A critique of the empirical claims and advocacy agenda. *Peabody Journal of Education, 32*(6), 283–295.

Lubienski, C., & Weitzel, P. (Eds.). (2010). *The charter school experiment: Expectations, evidence, and implications.* Harvard Education Press.

NCES. (n.d.). *Public school expenditures.* Retrieved April 10, 2020, from https://nces.ed.gov/programs/coe/indicator_cmb.asp

Ray, B. D. (2009a). *Homeschool progress report 2009: Academic achievement and demographics.* Home School Legal Defense Association. https://eric.ed.gov/?id=ED535134

Ray, B. D. (2009b). *Homeschooling across America: Academic achievement and demographic characteristics.* Retrieved August 5, 2019, from https://www.nheri.org/homeschooling-across-america-academic-achievement-and-demographic-characteristics/

Ray, B. D. (2015). *Research facts on homeschooling.* National Home Education Research Institute. http://www.nheri.org/ResearchFacts.pdf

Ray, B. D. (2019). *Research facts on homeschooling.* Retrieved August 5, 2019, from https://www.nheri.org/research-facts-on-homeschooling/

Rothstein, R. (2004). *Class and schools: Using social, economic, and educational reform to close the Black-White achievement gap.* Economic Policy Institute.

Seeking Alpha. (2019). *Median household income in January 2019.* Retrieved August 5, 2019, from https://seekingalpha.com/article/4244715-median-household-income-january-2019

U.S. Inflation Calculator. (n.d.). *Inflation calculator.* Retrieved August 5, 2019, from https://www.usinflationcalculator.com

Wilkinson, R., & Pickett, K. (2010). *The spirit level: Why greater equality makes societies stronger.* Bloomsbury Press.

CHAPTER 7

# Other Rationales & Conclusions

I have chosen, in this text, to highlight as separate chapters those rationales and justifications for homeschooling to those that are based on religious and/ or political ideologies as well as those using the effective and efficiency arguments. As noted in Chapter 1, the reasons, motivations, rationales, and justifications for choosing to educate a child at home rather than a traditional public school or other form of schooling are quite varied and are rarely singular in nature. And while the broad categories of religion, politics, effectiveness, and efficiency are overt categorizations, I have chosen here to combine other rationales here. Again, it is important to keep in mind that rationales are complex, these groupings are primarily in consideration of length, and these rationales, too, are not exhaustive. If there are three million families homeschooling, there are likely three million different, individual and context-specific, rationales for why they chose to homeschool.

One of the most-cited rationales provided for homeschooling centers around perceptions that the public school curriculum/environment is not ideal for a child. This rationale is quite broad in nature and can include, for example, pure disagreements with a particular set of curriculum approaches from a subject-matter perspective (e.g., how the Civil War is discussed) but such a disposition or orientation to the content may have an underlying political ideology. Additionally, concerns about the curriculum/environment may also be animated by underlying religious dogma and ideology. So, while concern for the "school environment" may be an oft-cited reason for homeschooling, I argue here that such rationales are not an exclusive category on their own. Though, from the same 100 Reasons to Homeschool list referenced in previous chapters, there are a few remaining that are not so easily categories into broad categories and can be considered culture and lifestyle rationales. Those are:

1. One -quarter of today's homeschoolers are Hispanic-Americans who want to preserve bilingualism and family culture.
2. Some families of color are choosing homeschooling to escape what they see as poor academic outcomes in schools, a curriculum that ignores their cultural heritage, institutional racism, and disciplinary approaches that disproportionately target children of color.
3. While the majority of homeschoolers are Christians, many Muslim families are choosing to homeschool, as are atheists.
4. With homeschooling, you can inspire your kids to love reading.

© KONINKLIJKE BRILL NV, LEIDEN, 2021 | DOI: 10.1163/9789004457096_007

OTHER RATIONALES & CONCLUSIONS

5. Maybe that's because they will actually read books, something one-quarter of Americans reported not doing in 2014.
6. Your kids might even choose to voluntarily read financial statements or do worksheets.
7. Parents can focus family learning around their own values, not someone else's.
8. Your kids may be happier.
9. YOU may be happier! All that time spent on your kids' homework can now be used more productively for family learning and living.
10. You can still work and homeschool.
11. And even grow a successful business while homeschooling your kids.
12. Your kids can also build successful businesses, as many grown unschoolers become entrepreneurs.
13. You can be a single parent and homeschool your kids.
14. More military families are choosing homeschooling to provide stability and consistency through frequent relocations and deployments.
15. Some kids are asking to be homeschooled.
16. And they may even thank you for it.
17. Homeschooling can create strong sibling relationships and tight family bonds. (McDonald, 2019)

Again, some of these rationales approach homeschooling over public school attendance as a this or that proposition rather than a this and that proposition. For example, the first one listed above about maintaining bilingualism is decidedly misleading since, presumably, attendance at a public school using English as the dominant language and Spanish being used at home would be the practice through which children would build and maintain bilingualism. Attending public schools that utilize English does not impede a family's ability to practice other languages at home to ensure that children develop in a bilingual family. Moreover, the rise of dual-language immersion programs in public schools quite possibly provide a more professional approach for students to become bi- or trilingual. Either way, the sheltering of children at home to preserve family language (which is a vitally important and laudable aim) is less likely to support bilingualism as much as enrollment in public schools would. Additionally, those rationales above such as homeschooling so that you can "inspire your kids to love reading" represent a false binary where homeschooling is understood as affording the opportunity to help children learn to read and, by default, such a love of reading is not able to be produced by attending public schools – generally speaking – but also not able to be done with a combination of public schools and parental influence on reading habits at home. This is reinforced by the subsequent rationale that suggests that kids in public schools simply do not read and that the only solution for such low readership levels among *all* Americans is to homeschool.

To the second rationale raised above as it relates to perceptions of systemic failures on part of the public school systems to provide adequate and equal educative opportunities for all students – namely students of color and those coming from lower socioeconomic status families – is, without a doubt, an important concern and one that public scholars and activists have taken up as a cause célèbre for decades. Yet, given the financial barriers associated with homeschooling (see Chapter 6), the racial minority families that are able to "escape" those public schools are the ones who can afford to do so, thus exacerbating the downward spiral of funding and community investment in those public schools. Improvements in representative curriculum and culturally responsive pedagogy are, with absolutely no doubt, areas of improvement for public schools. And, despite slow progress (often hampered by the very policy forces pushing to stymie public schools to promote privatization), improvements are happening and the parents who have the social and cultural capital required to pull their children out of public schools to provide such educative experiences for their individual children, could conversely advocate for those changes at the local and systemic levels.

To the final point above, it is entirely possible that spending time together as a family, 24/7, can lead to stronger sibling relationships. What is not mentioned, however, is that the opposite is also quite possible. To that point, the increased quarantining of the family unit can lead to an increase in domestic violence as was seen during the national quarantine during the COVID-19 pandemic (Taub, 2020) to the point that the Council on Foreign Relations suggested the rise of domestic violence "particularly among marginalized populations" represents a double-pandemic (Bettinger-Lopez, 2020). Moreover, while child safety as a result of perceived negative or unsafe school environments can be a rationale to homeschool, having guns in the home is associated with a sharp increase of the risk of fatal violence (Faria, 2001; Metzl, 2019) and increased presence around such homes can be associated with an increase in accidents. And, as was explicated in Chapter 2 child abuse and neglect remain an important consideration surrounding homeschooling. Not because homeschooling, as a practice, is naturally associated with higher rates but that a huge portion of abuse and neglect cases are discovered as a result of children attending public schools where the employees are mandated reporters. In fact, during the COVID-19 pandemic quarantine, reports of child abuse decreased by *half*

OTHER RATIONALES & CONCLUSIONS

since schools closed (Prabhu, 2020). So, while it is entirely possible that stronger family bonds can be sculpted from a homeschooling experience, it is also possible that the practice can help camouflage unhealthy family relationships.

Drawing again from the same list of 100 reasons to homeschool, other rationales can be categorized as related to medical or developmental claims include:

1. Issues like ADHD might disappear or become less problematic.
2. It doesn't matter if they fidget.
3. Your kids can be little for longer. Early school enrollment has been linked by Harvard researchers with troubling rates of ADHD diagnosis. A year can make a big difference in early childhood development.
4. Some of us are just late bloomers. We don't all need to be on "America's early-blooming conveyor belt."
5. Then again, homeschooling can help those kids who might be early bloomers and graduate from college at 16.
6. Adolescent anxiety, depression, and suicide decline during the summer, but Vanderbilt University researchers found that suicidal tendencies spike at back-to-school time. (This is a pattern opposite to that of adults, who experience more suicidal thoughts and acts in the summertime.) Homeschooling your kids may reduce these school-induced mental health issues.
7. Your kids can have healthier lunches than they would at school.
8. Research shows that teen homeschoolers get more sleep than their schooled peers.
9. Homeschooling may be particularly helpful for children with disabilities, like dyslexia, as the personalized learning model allows for more flexibility and customization. (McDonald, 2019)

First, serious medical and behavioral conditions such as ADHD do not appear or disappear on a whim. Nor does the prevalence of such conditions vary due to contextual settings. While there is some suggestion that ADHD may be over-diagnosed (Lane, 2017; Merten, Cwik, Margraf, & Schneider, 2017), not attending public schools where trained special education teachers and school psychologists have the capability to diagnose such conditions does not mean that ADHD will disappear. In many ways, the first three rationales above related to ADHD would seem to suggest that if a student avoids public schools, they will avoid being diagnosed and, therefore, do not have ADHD. An avoidance of an issue does not make the issue less of an issue for students. Also above are spurious correlations surrounding timing of the year and suicide rates as well as claims about lunches. This is, again, a false binary as the lunch that students can have at home (via homeschool) are the exact same lunch they can have at school should they bring their own lunches. Moreover, federal efforts have made dramatic improvements on nutritional standards of school lunches despite conservative and libertarian efforts to eliminate them out of political spite (U.S. Department of Agriculture, 2017). Akin to the anti-intellectual claims rampant in the homeschooling community, it is dangerous to claim that a homeschooling parent with less than a high school diploma is adequately trained in diagnosing and treating disabilities, like dyslexia and ADHD, as is claimed above.

Finally, there are the "since other people are doing it with growing popularity, you should too" rationales:

1.  You're not alone. Nearly two million US children are homeschooled, and the homeschooling population is increasingly reflective of America's diversity. In fact, the number of black homeschoolers doubled between 2007 and 2011.
2.  Homeschooling is growing in popularity worldwide, especially in India, Australia, the United Kingdom, Israel, and even in China, where it's illegal.
3.  Throughout the American colonial and revolutionary eras, homeschooling was the norm, educating leaders like George Washington and Abigail Adams.
4.  In fact, many famous people were homeschooled.
5.  And many famous people homeschool their own kids.
6.  Homeschooling is legal in all 50 US states and has been since 1993, but regulations vary widely by state. (McDonald, 2019)

## 1    So, What Follows?

First, I want to again be clear that there should be limited reason to suspect that the choices that parents make about the wellbeing and the education of their children are done so out of malicious intent. Of course, there are instances where malicious intent exists and nefarious and damaging actions occur (and there are ways in which homeschooling can hide some manifestations of that) but, broadly, parents want what is best for their children. Yet, in some ways, this disposition can cloud our collective obligation to children – namely, other people's children. We all benefit from an educated populace and it is well within the interest of the nation to ensure that future generations receive ample and equitable education if they, and we, are to survive and thrive not

OTHER RATIONALES & CONCLUSIONS

just as a nation, but as a species. We must understand the growth and development of children as a process and aim not removed from ourselves and society but, rather, intimately tied to one another. The academic growth and self-actualization of my neighbor's children bears fruit for our entire community. To this, we must reinvest ourselves. Homeschooling, on the contrary, reimagines this social connective tissue and divests from the collective good in theory and in practice. In the era of the 2020 Presidential election that brought with it an immense amount of political and social discord and the raging COVID-19 pandemic, what we need is *more* civil and civic engagement, not less. *More* collective education, not less. *More* collective efforts, not individualization.

Yet, despite all of this, the reasons for the growth of homeschooling across the United States over the past few decades relies, primarily, on claims of effectiveness and efficiencies (of which I have addressed in this text) against the backdrop of notions of American rugged individualism often animated by deeply held religious or political views. As organizations like the HSLDA and conservative policymakers continue to push for the expansion of the defunding of public schools in favor of market-oriented educational reforms including vouchers for private schools and homeschooling (Brewer, 2020), it highlights the need for a critical, and social, analysis of how we operate the functional cornerstone of our democracy: schools. The practice of homeschooling is, in my view, the epitome of schooling-as-individualism. And, as it may be apparent, democracy requires a collective obligation to each other and our future generations. In practice, collective democracy cannot realize its full potential through a practice of individualism and isolated silos of echo chambers of religion and political doctrine. The sweeping damage of the COVID-19 pandemic that wrought havoc to the economy and death to hundreds of thousands gave us all the opportunity to celebrate our shared obligation to one another and this obligation should include a (re)commitment to providing equitable educative opportunities for our nation's students and broad social justice for all. We must seek ways to bolster our public schooling system, expand our recruitment of teachers to include a more diverse representation of our nation's schoolchildren and communities, increase our funding of public schools and all manner of public services. While there will likely never be an end to private, individualized, religious/political, and classist homeschooling, we can continue to focus on the necessary reforms to public schools to pave the way for this, and future, generations. We are all in this together, our schools and the education of our children should be no different. As an educator to millions of children, Fred Rogers taught us that, "we live in a world in which we need to share responsibility. It's easy to say, 'It's not my child, not my community, not my world, not my problem.' Then there are those who see the need and respond. I consider those people my heroes." Public school teachers live this creed, and again, this book is dedicated to them.

### References

Bettinger-Lopez, C. (2020). *A double pandemic: Domestic violence in the age of Covid-19.* Retrieved May 15, 2020, from https://www.cfr.org/in-brief/double-pandemic-domestic-violence-age-covid-19

Brewer, T. J. (2020). *Opinion: Ballot question reveals Republican zeal for school vouchers.* Retrieved May 19, 2020, from https://www.ajc.com/blog/get-schooled/opinion-ballot-question-reveals-republican-zeal-for-school-vouchers/ TCduuokU67ZINPPtzGZYTI/?fbclid=IwAR1sjxBxrKnD6BrDmLOhaM 16qxgznbxwuaoUHMCtaqbzleakNq5Dv6dgSWk

Faria, M. A. (2001). *The tainted public-health model of gun control.* Retrieved July 1, 2019, from https://fee.org/articles/the-tainted-public-health-model-of-gun-control/

Lane, C. (2017). *ADHD is now widely overdiagnosed and for multiple reasons.* Retrieved May 15, 2020, from https://www.psychologytoday.com/us/blog/side-effects/201710/adhd-is-now-widely-overdiagnosed-and-multiple-reasons

McDonald, K. (2019). *100 reasons to homeschool your kids.* Retrieved July 8, 2019, from https://fee.org/articles/100-reasons-to-homeschool-your-kids/

Merten, E. C., Cwik, J. C., Margraf, J., & Schneider, S. (2017). Overdiagnosis of mental disorders in children and adolescents (in developed countries). *Child and Adolescent Psychiatry and Mental Health, 11*(5), 1–11.

Metzl, J. M. (2019). *Dying of Whiteness: How the politics of racial resentment is killing America's heartland.* Basic Books.

Prabhu, M. T. (2020). *Child abuse reporting in Georgia down by half since schools closed amid virus.* Retrieved April 16, 2020, from https://www.ajc.com/news/state—regional-govt—politics/child-abuse-reporting-georgia-down-half-since-schools-closed-amid-virus/RKg3HzBy86Ai3QNq3jrZML/

Taub, A. (2020). *A new Covid-19 crisis: Domestic abuse rises worldwide.* Retrieved May 15, 2020, from https://www.nytimes.com/2020/04/06/world/coronavirus-domestic-violence.html

U.S. Department of Agriculture. (2017). *Ag secretary Perdue moves to make school meals great again.* Retrieved May 15, 2020, from https://www.usda.gov/media/press-releases/2017/05/01/ag-secretary-perdue-moves-make-school-meals-great-again

# Index

19 Kids and Counting   55

abuse   2, 7, 15, 26, 27, 98
academic outcomes   9, 10, 74, 77–79, 81, 82, 88, 91, 92
Attention Deficit Hyperactivity Disorder (ADHD)   99, 100
anti-intellectualism   3, 41, 56, 57
anti-science   58

Beecher, Catherine   29
Bible   24, 29, 30, 50, 51, 53, 58, 59, 61, 71, 72
Black   8, 82, 100

Council for the Accreditation of Educator Preparation (CAEP)   29
capitalism   22, 23, 27, 28, 65, 71
Center for Disease Control (CDC)   3, 23, 24
charter schools   3–5, 12, 22, 50, 69, 77, 87
child abuse   15, 26, 27, 98
Christian   22–25, 50–56, 58–60, 62, 67, 68, 71, 72, 96
Christian reconstructionism   51
collective   2–5, 19, 28, 65, 71, 77, 88, 100, 101
conservative   6, 22, 24, 28, 44, 50–53, 55, 67, 100, 101
cost   5, 12–14, 71, 75, 85–92
COVID-19   14, 15, 27, 98, 101
Culture War   53, 54

De Vos, Betsy   50, 52, 54
Dunbar, Cynthia   50, 54, 55, 72
Duncan, Arne   22

effectiveness   9, 16, 19, 71, 74, 76, 80, 96, 101
efficiency   19, 71, 85, 89, 92, 96
English   97
Establishment Clause   13
evolution   18, 50, 55, 56, 58, 59, 65

finance   5, 14, 31, 45, 65, 69, 77, 82, 89, 90–92, 97, 98
Fox, Megan   56, 57, 60
Friedman, Milton   22, 66, 87, 89

guns   25, 67, 98

Hispanic   8, 96
Home School Legal Defense Association (HSLDA)   6, 26, 41, 53, 54, 85, 92, 101

income   10, 12, 14, 15, 45, 78, 82, 87–89
individual   2–5, 12, 13, 19, 28, 30, 33–35, 44, 45, 65, 71, 79–81, 87–90, 96, 98, 101
individualized   6, 7, 19, 45, 75, 90, 101

kindergarten   9, 43, 44

libertarian   66, 71, 72, 86, 100

Mann, Horace   2, 35, 42
market   6, 28, 71, 86, 87, 101
meritocracy   4, 71, 77, 86
money   13, 14, 71, 79, 89, 90, 92
Muslim   52, 60, 96

National Council for Accreditation of Teacher Education (NCATE)   29
National Home Education Research Institute (NHERI)   6, 7, 9, 10, 66, 87–89, 91

Obama, Barack   50, 60
online   3, 12, 14, 41, 59, 61, 75

parent sovereignty   1, 2, 13, 18, 19, 31, 32, 41, 42
personalized   68, 80, 99
profession/professional/professionalization   1–3, 14, 15, 19, 29, 31–36, 38–42, 80, 85, 91, 97
protestant   50, 51, 60, 62, 67, 71, 72
public school   9, 10, 12, 13, 25–28, 37, 38, 40, 41, 43–45, 51, 60, 61, 71, 76, 78, 79, 81, 82, 85, 86, 88–92, 96–98, 102

quiverfull   10, 51, 52, 55

regulate/regulation   7, 26, 27, 29, 31, 65, 70, 71, 100
Republican   53, 54

SAT scores   77
school choice   3, 12–14, 40, 45, 70–72, 77, 89, 90

school vouchers   13, 70
sex education   19, 24, 55
sovereignty   1, 2, 13, 18, 19, 31, 32, 41, 42
Special Education   99
Stewart, Katherine   24, 51, 52, 72

TurningPoint USA   27

vaccine/anti-vaccine   3, 18, 40, 41, 43, 50–52,
      55, 67, 82

White   7, 8, 45